WRITERS AND THE

ISOBEL ARMSTR
General Edit

BRYAN LOUGH
Advisory Edi

J. G. Ballard

J. G. BALLARD
photograph by kind permission of J. G. Ballard

WW

J. G. BALLARD

MICHEL DELVILLE

Northcote House
in association with the
British Council

for Elisabeth

© Copyright 1998 by Michel Delville

First published in 1998 by Northcote House Publishers Ltd, Plymbridge House, Estover Road, Plymouth PL6 7PY, United Kingdom.
Tel: +44 (01752) 202368 Fax: +44 (01752) 202330.

British Library Cataloguing-in-Publication Data
A catalogue record for this book is available from the British Library

ISBN 0-7463-0867-1

Typeset by PDQ Typesetting, Newcastle-under-Lyme
Printed and bound in the United Kingdom

Contents

Acknowledgements

Grateful thanks are due to Andrew Norris, who gave the manuscript careful reading and made many helpful suggestions. I would also like to express my gratitude to the Belgian National Fund for Scientific Research for financial support while I was researching and writing this study.

Biographical Outline

1930   James Graham Ballard born on 15 November in Shanghai, China, the son of a managing director for a subsidiary of a Manchester textile firm.

1942–5   Interned in the POW camp of Lunghua, near Shanghai.

1946   Arrives in England.

1946–9   Attends Leys School, Cambridge.

1949–51   Reads medicine at King's College, Cambridge University, with the intention of becoming a psychiatrist.

1952   Leaves King's College for the University of London where he switches from medicine to English.

1953–4   Abandons his studies altogether and, after taking a series of odd jobs, joins the Royal Air Force for a two-year voluntary Short Service Commission partly spent in Moosejaw, Canada.

1955   Marries Helen Mary Matthews.

1956   Birth of first child, James Christopher.
            Publishes his first science fiction story, 'Escapement', in the December 1956 issue of *New Worlds*.

1957   Birth of second child, Fay.

1957–61   Works as an editor of the periodical, *Chemistry and Industry*.

1959   Birth of third child, Beatrice.

1962   Publishes first novel, *The Wind from Nowhere*, and becomes a full-time writer.
            The Drowned World, The Voices of Time.

1963   *The Four-Dimensional Nightmare.*

1964   Death of Helen Mary Ballard.
            The Burning World (retitled *The Drought*), *The Terminal Beach.*

1966   *The Crystal World, The Impossible Man.*

1967   *The Day of Forever, The Disaster Area, The Overloaded Man.*

1970   *The Atrocity Exhibition.* Crashed car exhibition held at the London New Arts Laboratory.

1971   *Vermilion Sands.*

1972   *Chronopolis.*

1973   *Crash.*

1974   *Concrete Island.*

1975   *High-Rise.*

1976   *Low-Flying Aircraft.*

1979   *The Unlimited Dream Company,* winner of the British Science Fiction Award.

1981   *Hello America.*

1982   *Myths of the Near Future.*

1984   *Empire of the Sun* wins the *Guardian* Fiction Prize and the James Tait Black Memorial Prize, and is short-listed for the Booker Prize.

1987   *The Day of Creation.*
Cameo appearance in Steven Spielberg's film version of *Empire of the Sun* (screenplay by Tom Stoppard).

1988   *Running Wild.*

1990   *War Fever.*

1991   *The Kindness of Women,* 'sequel' to *Empire of the Sun.*

1994   *Rushing to Paradise.*

1996   Attends the premiere of Steven Cronenberg's film version of *Crash* at the Cannes Film Festival.
A User's Guide to the Millenium.
Cocaine Nights.

Abbreviations and References

Page references to Ballard's works are to the following editions.

AE	*The Atrocity Exhibition* (revised edition; London: Flamingo, 1993)
BSS	*The Best Short Stories of J. G. Ballard* (New York: Holt, 1978)
C.	*Crash* (New York: The Noonday Press, 1994)
CI	*Concrete Island* (London: Triad/Granada, 1985)
CN	*Cocaine Nights* (London: Flamingo, 1996)
CW	*The Crystal World* (New York: Farrar, Straus and Giroux, 1988)
D.	*The Drought* (London: Panther/Triad, 1978)
DA	*The Disaster Area* (London: Flamingo, 1992)
DC	*The Day of Creation* (London: Flamingo, 1993)
DF	*The Day of Forever* (London: Flamingo, 1995)
DW	*The Drowned World* (London: Dent, 1983)
ES	*Empire of the Sun* (London: Flamingo, 1994)
Foreword	Foreword to Aldous Huxley's *The Doors of Perception* (London: Flamingo, 1994)
HA	*Hello America* (New York: Carroll & Graf, 1989)
HR	*High-Rise* (New York: Carroll & Graf, 1975)
KW	*The Kindness of Women* (London: HarperCollins, 1991)
LFA	*Low-Flying Aircraft* (London: Flamingo, 1992)
MNF	*Myths of the Near Future* (London: Vintage, 1994)
RP	*Rushing to Paradise* (London: Flamingo, 1994)
R/S	*RE/Search*, 8–9 (1984). Special J. G. Ballard issue.
RW	*Running Wild* (London: Hutchinson, 1988)
TB	*The Terminal Beach* (London: Gollancz, 1964, 1993)
UDC	*The Unlimited Dream Company* (London: Flamingo, 1992)

UGM	*A User's Guide to the Millenium* (London: Harper-Collins, 1996)
VH	*The Venus Hunters* (London: Flamingo, 1992)
VS	*Vermilion Sands* (New York: Carroll & Graf, 1988)
VT	*The Voices of Time* (New York: Berkley, 1962)
WF	*War Fever* (London: Paladin, 1991)

1

Introduction

At least three J. G. Ballards have so far been championed in critical studies and literary histories: the science fiction writer, famous for his disaster novels and stories of entropic dissolution; the admirer of William S. Burroughs and author of scandalous tales remarkable for their sexual frankness and eccentric violence; and the Booker Prize nominee, whose account of a boy's life in Japanese-occupied wartime Shanghai in *Empire of the Sun* was published to great acclaim in 1984. The first of these has been abundantly described and publicized as one of the leading representatives of the New Wave school of British science fiction. During the 1960s, he became one of the leading contributors to Michael Moorcock's seminal magazine, *New Worlds*,[1] which advocated a wider range of subject matter and the use of experimental forms and techniques in order to endow the genre with 'literary' value. By 1966, Ballard had already published four novels and more than fifty short stories which succeeded in raising the genre to a high literary standard, at a time when it was dismissed as adolescent, escapist and, ultimately, second-rate art.

Ballard's first four science fiction novels, *The Wind from Nowhere, The Drowned World, The Drought* and *The Crystal World*, are now recognized as superlative work even outside the circles of SF aficionados. His second phase began in the early 1970s, when he was turned into a cult figure of the 'underground' scene as the author of *The Atrocity Exhibition* and the 'pre-cyberpunk' novel *Crash*. A few years later, he became interested in the more regenerative landscapes of the dream-allegory (*The Unlimited Dream Company*). To make things even more complicated, *Empire of the Sun* – Ballard's more recent swerve away from both SF and avant-garde fiction towards the more familiar realms of the semi-autobiographical novel – established his reputation as a 'mainstream' author.

Ballard's reputation as a novelist has increased steadily over the years and has now outgrown his initial achievements as a 'genre' writer. However, it was not until the publication of *Empire of the Sun* – which won the *Guardian* Fiction Prize and the James Tait Black Memorial Prize, and was shortlisted for the Booker Prize – that he began to be recognized as a major contemporary English novelist by the critical establishment. There is no doubt that the recognition brought to Ballard by *Empire of the Sun* and its subsequent filmed version prompted a reappraisal of his earlier works, most of which were reprinted in paperback editions following the success of Spielberg's movie. Long before the critical and commercial watershed marked by *Empire of the Sun*, however, Ballard's imaginative powers and the originality of his fiction had already won him the admiration of a broad and international readership, as well as that of numerous leading contemporary writers such as Graham Greene, William S. Burroughs, Angela Carter, Michael Moorcock, Martin Amis, William Boyd, Anthony Burgess, Susan Sontag, Brian Aldiss, Fredric Jameson and, lastly, Jean Baudrillard, whose writings, as we will see, often appear as a theoretical counterpart to Ballard's fictional world.

As the following chapters will demonstrate, Ballard's fiction – which reconciles critical and commercial recognition, far-out experimentalism and the conventions of popular fiction – does not let itself be assimilated to traditional generic categories, either within or outside the boundaries of so-called 'genre' fiction. Ballard's ambiguous position as a novelist writing across high and low, literary and popular paradigms (a profile he shares with a several other New Wave pioneers such as Brian Aldiss, Samuel R. Delany and Michael Moorcock) has also had the more unfortunate effect of relegating his work to the margins of both the SF canon and the literary establishment. His refusal to play into the conventions of straight, popular SF and his subsequent turn, in the early 1970s, to a more serious kind of 'speculative' fiction have indeed tended to alienate a substantial part of the science fiction 'fandom' which constituted the bulk of Ballard's audience in the 1960s and early 1970s. Because they contain little reference to the codified frameworks of genre fiction, his most recent novels, in particular, are considered of marginal interest by many science fiction readers.[2]

Still, one must resist the temptation to draw a clear-cut line between Ballard's 'ambitious' SF novels and short stories and his more mainstream writings. Nor should one read his career as a long process of artistic maturation that eventually enabled him to disentangle himself from the conventions of genre fiction. Such simplified accounts of the evolution of Ballard's work disregard the fact that the early science fiction stories abound in motifs and obsessions that return to haunt such later works as *Empire of the Sun* and *The Kindness of Women* – Ballard belongs in fact to that category of writers who are engaged in a constant revision of a number of recurrent modes and themes which, in different forms, survive and transcend each 'period' of his work. Ballard himself sees his SF and mainstream works as part of the same attempt to expand the field of expertise of fiction writing. He has also repeatedly argued that science fiction was a means to an end, rather than a mere set of generic and narrative conventions. Accordingly, he has suggested that science fiction should no longer be preoccupied exclusively with the future of mankind and should become, instead, increasingly concerned with how to make sense of our present circumstances and investigate the specific vocabulary and mythologies of the contemporary experience. It therefore fulfils an essential role in exploring the furthest reaches of the psychology of modern man and in providing a forum for a number of issues usually neglected by traditional, realist fiction. 'However naively', Ballard wrote recently, '[science fiction] has tried to respond to the most significant events of our time – the threat of nuclear war, over-population, the computer revolution, the possibilities and abuses of medical science, the ecological dangers to our planet, the consumer society as benign tyranny – topics that haunt our minds but are scarcely considered by the mainstream novel' (*UGM* 194).

As we will see, Ballard's own achievement as a fiction writer and commentator on contemporary culture embodies a comprehensive understanding of a number of basic conflicts and contradictions underlying Western societies – contradictions that often tie in with the proliferation of mass-produced images and the ensuing disappearance of the real which the author sees as resulting from the widespread influence of electronic media technologies. In his oft-quoted introduction to the French edition of *Crash*, first published in 1974, Ballard comments that 'the balance between fiction and reality has changed significantly in the past decade':

> We live in a world ruled by fictions of every kind: mass merchandising, advertising, politics considered as a branch of advertising, the instant translation of science and technology into popular imagery, the increasing blurring and intermingling of identities within the realm of consumer goods, the pre-empting of any free or imaginative response to experience by the television screen. We live inside an enormous novel. For the writer in particular it is less and less necessary for him to invent the fictional content of his novel. The fiction is already there. The writer's task is to invent reality. (*R/S* 97–8)

In many respects, Ballard's oeuvre seems informed by a recognition that no stable representation can result from the jumble of material and ideological elements that constitute contemporary culture. According to such a view, it is no longer possible to do justice to the peculiar logic of the late twentieth century by resorting to conventional narrative strategies that deny what some have come to see as the lack of autonomy and the increasingly fluid nature of selfhood in the postindustrial age. People who expect such traditional conventions will be immediately disoriented by Ballard's obsession with extreme forms of psychological isolation, his interest in types, rather than characters, as well as his penchant for allegories or visions, rather than stories or 'plots'. More than forty years after the publication of his first short story, Ballard indeed remains one of the most controversial presences in contemporary British fiction. His compulsion to write unflinchingly on matters of sexual perversion, entropy, alienation and death, in particular, has puzzled, and sometimes discouraged, many readers, reviewers and publishers who have questioned the integrity of his fiction, both from an aesthetic and from a moral point of view. Whereas Duncan Fallowell, for instance, has deplored Ballard's tendency to write about 'a dehumanized world of helpless ill-fortune',[3] other critics, such as Robert Platzner, have accused him of political and moral nihilism. Platzner's criticism is also directed against Ballard's tendency to indulge in 'apocalyptic anxieties'.[4]

His complaints focus primarily on what he sees as Ballard's attempts, in *The Atrocity Exhibition*, to 'fill [the] vacuum [of mental space] with the debris of contemporary American politics and pop culture perceived exclusively from the perspective of conspiracy theory and paranoia'.[5] 'The sheer hopelessness of Ballard's metamorphic future (or fantasied present)', he concludes, 'expresses only his conviction that modern life offers no resistance to the self-shattering force of total doubt'.[6]

What Fallowell's and Platzner's objections have in common is the allegation that Ballard's fiction suffers from a lack of moral and emotional commitment. It is evidently pointless to deny that Ballard's talents lie in the sustained power of imagery and ideas, rather than in the realist description of people and relationships. It is also true that Ballard's novels and short stories often enact a radically desensitized response to life, tinged with a certain amount of Freudian determinism that substitutes the primacy of unconscious drives for traditional (some will say 'humanist') notions of conscious motivation and individual autonomy. This particular feature of his work, however, can be accounted for not by a lack of 'technical' skill or moral integrity but by a deliberate attempt to depict a society which is essentially post-emotional, one in which human beings emerge as strangely distanced and detached observers of their own affectless condition. The issue of whether Ballard's fiction can truly be considered as pessimistic or nihilistic will be discussed in the following chapters. One may point out, at this stage, that Platzner's criticism of Ballard's apocalyptic strategies screens off the many ways in which Ballard's fiction is as concerned with the possibility of self-fulfilment and spiritual regeneration, as well as with the healing powers of the imagination, as it is preoccupied with violence, regression and the entropic dissolution of society and the individual.

The point is that one cannot come to terms with Ballard's fiction unless one is prepared to plunge immediately into complexity and paradox. By opting for the violent, radical aesthetic of what he himself calls his 'library of extreme metaphors' (*KW* 342), Ballard harnesses the nexus of powers and forces unleashed within the most idiosyncratic obsessions of modern man. In this respect, his 'myths of the near future' –

most of which are based on the postulate that sex, violence, technology and politics are necessarily intertwined – can be construed as a literary counterpart to a line of thought which, from Georges Bataille's 'accursed share' to Gilles Deleuze and Félix Guattari's 'schizoanalysis', centres on the interpenetration of libidinal, psychological and political energies and, thereby, seeks to overturn our most fundamental notions of social and aesthetic representation. In doing so, Ballard's fiction is able to address fundamental issues about contemporary Western societies – issues raised by the cultural interface between the subjective and the objective (or, in more Ballardian terms, between 'inner' and 'outer' landscapes), as well as between the personal and the ideological. Perhaps more importantly, Ballard's work acts as a forum for contemporary debates about regression, sexual deviance and the role of violence and radicalism in the arts. Furthermore, it demonstrates how such subjects can be discussed in a way that is at once critical and humorous, as well as simultaneously analytical and imaginative.

In a time of acute sexual, social and cultural anxiety, Ballard's obsessions are too violent to be ignored. Informed by an awareness of how identity is shaped through memory and repetition and a recognition that the human mind is the site of complex, and often conflicting, needs that alternate between extreme forms of abjection and spirituality, they are prepared to shred the fabric of our most cherished notions of self and reality and oblige us to contemplate the uncertain terrain of our 'millenial hopes and fears' (MNF, p. v). Ballard brings to this exploration a full recognition of the complexity of contemporary political agendas, as well as his own unmistakable style, which alternates between the bald and the baroque, the clinical sanity of the scientist and the raw, convulsive energy of Surrealism.

2

The Nature of the Catastrophe

Ballard's first four science fiction novels, *The Wind from Nowhere* (1962), *The Drowned World* (1962), *The Drought* (1965) and *The Crystal World* (1966), all involve a drastic change in the global climate threatening to bring about the collapse of modern civilization. They therefore subscribe, at least superficially, to the conventions of what was then a most popular subgenre of science fiction: the so-called 'disaster story'. Even though it is clearly indebted to a tradition of British catastrophe stories that includes such apocalyptic 'classics' as John Wyndham's *Revolt of the Triffids* (1952) and John Christopher's *The Death of Grass* (1956), Ballard's early fiction differs from the plethora of disaster tales published at the time in various SF and pulp magazines, in that it focuses less on the disaster itself than on the characters' various mental and physical adjustments to it. Ballard's novels – which are entirely devoid of the scenes of private and collective panic which we usually associate with the genre – also mark a decided departure from the most basic ideological assumptions of the disaster tale, whose main emphasis had until then been on a small group of survivors and their heroic attempts to overcome the crisis and restore a new sense of social and political normalcy. This particular aspect of Ballard's fiction is most apparent in his second novel, *The Drowned World* (published shortly after *The Wind from Nowhere*, a hastily written apocalypse story later disowned by its author), in which the whole planet is reverting to prehistoric tropical times as a result of a sudden temperature increase caused by solar storms. The protagonist, Dr Robert Kerans, is a member of a scientific expedition whose aim is to conduct a survey of the effects of these rapid rises in temperature on the environment and observe the progression of the new world of Triassic swamps and jungles. Kerans soon begins to perceive that the metamorphosis of his surroundings is paralleled by changes in his own psychic state and that of the other characters. He eventually comes to accept the new landscape of steaming jungles and mangroves as both the concrete affirmation of an unconscious desire of mankind and the sign of the emergence of a new personality in himself.

The steaming landscapes of Ballard's *The Drowned World*, as well as Kerans's final journey into the midst of the jungle, invite a comparison with Joseph Conrad's *Heart of Darkness*, another tale of spiritual initiation into the hidden powers of the subconscious involving direct correspondences between inner and outer landscapes. Unlike Marlow, however, whose psychological journey to the centre of the African continent is followed by a return to civilization, Kerans's quest is prompted by 'pre-uterine dreams' reflecting his 'unconscious acceptance of the logic of his own devolutionary descent' (*DW* 91, 113). This process of biological and psychic devolution can only lead to his death and final entropic dissolution into 'the archeopsychic zero' (*DW* 113).

Perhaps the most haunting quality of Ballard's narrative derives from the 'deepdreams' (*DW* 158) experienced by Kerans and the other characters in the novel. The impact of the 'deepdreams' on the characters' consciousnesses proves all the more powerful as it tends to erase the distinction between the real and the phantasmagoric, just as the latent and manifest contents of the dreams themselves are confused. As Dr Bodkin explains to Kerans, the visions they experience while sleeping are in fact so many manifestations of 'an ancient organic memory millions of years old' (*DW* 74). Of all the members of the expedition, only practical-minded Colonel Riggs can manage to resist the mesmerizing powers of the deepdreams by holding on to reason and logic and obeying instructions to the letter. As for Strangman, the Kurtz figure of the novel – described by Kerans as 'a white devil out of a voodoo cult' (*DW* 158) – he embodies the darker implications of the pre-rational realm of the phantasmagoric jungle. Significantly, his moral corruption and primitive savagery is associated with his attempts to pump out the lagoon and thereby reverse the ineluctable psycho-biological disruptions announced by the deepdreams.

Kerans is only one of the first in a long line of Ballardian protagonists – many of them scientists – who, instead of resisting the menace of an unprecedented environmental change, come to accept and even accelerate the effects of the global catastrophe. Indeed, many of Ballard's characters seem to respond to the threat by undergoing a transformation which reflects in psychological terms the external alterations to their world. In this respect, Kerans, like the protagonists of Ballard's other early novels and short stories, embodies different facets of a single figure which James Cawthorn named 'The Dissolving Hero'. 'Faced with the breakdown of the Universe', Cawthorn writes, Ballard's 'Dissolving Hero' 'does not fight, but instead seeks, literally, to be absorbed'.[1]

This particular feature of Ballard's devolutionary tales has aroused a considerable amount of critical controversy. Robert Platzner, for instance, has complained that Ballard's 'vision of irreversible, regressive transformation' has left him 'with very little to write about except the inhuman and the inorganic'.[2] Responding to such allegations of pessimism and nihilism, Ballard explains: 'My characters embrace what most people would run miles from, in novels like *The Drowned World*, *The Crystal World*, and in another way *Crash*... In many cases they embrace death, but that doesn't mean I am pessimistic... I think that all of my fiction is optimistic because it's a fiction of psychic fulfilment. The characters are finding themselves, which is after all the only definition of real happiness: to find yourself and be who you are...' (*R/S* 161). The revelatory nature and metamorphic implications of Kerans's journey are indeed clear from the very beginning of the novel when Kerans, wondering about 'the growing isolation and self-containment' exhibited by the other members of the expedition, is reminded of 'the slackening metabolism and biological withdrawal of all animal forms about to undergo a major metamorphosis': 'Sometimes he wondered what zone of transit he himself was entering, sure that his own withdrawal was symptomatic not of a dormant schizophrenia, but of a careful preparation for a radically new environment, with its own internal landscape and logic, where old categories of thought would merely be an encumbrance' (DW 14).

In a world gradually returning to its Mesozoic past, the last remnants of civilization represented by the surviving streets and buildings of the city of London – which are about to be submerged by vast malarial swamps and lagoons – seem anachronistic and unreal, 'like a reflection in a lake that has somehow lost its original' (DW 19). Kerans, who was born and raised in the Arctic Circle (now a subtropical area whose relatively mild climate makes it the only inhabitable place on earth), is too young to have experienced life in the Western cities at first hand and therefore remains indifferent to their ultimate downfall. Later, the full significance of Kerans's epiphany becomes apparent as the blinding sunlight 'bathing the submerged levels below his consciousness' carries him 'downwards into the warm pellucid depths where the nominal realities of time and space ceased to exist' (DW 83). Having shed any sense of himself as an individual being, Kerans eventually becomes 'a second Adam searching for the forgotten paradises of the reborn sun' (DW 175), an archetypal figure standing for mankind's longing for a prelapsarian state.

The Drought and The Crystal World are two other stories of literal and metaphorical devolution that elaborate on the basic themes and motifs developed in The Drowned World. The cataclysmic premises of the first novel are brought about by a worldwide drought caused by industrial pollution of the seas. The story as a whole focuses on the journey undertaken by Dr Ransom from the inland city of Mount Royal to the seashore and ends with his return to Mount Royal ten years later. Like Kerans's quest in The Drowned World, Ransom's journey to the sea coast is deeply and consistently symbolical of a journey into the depths of the inner self – a mental pilgrimage in which each individual event, encounter or set of circumstances invariably signifies a second order of correlated meanings whose universal resonance is reinforced by a number of biblical references and literary allusions ranging from Coleridge's 'Rime of the Ancient Mariner' to Shakespeare's The Tempest. Ballard's sandy wastes, in particular, come to be seen as visible manifestations of an invisible order of things, one which reflects his ongoing interest in correspondences between the phenomenal world and the inner landscapes of the unconscious and subconscious mind.

One of Ballard's most memorable landscapes in *The Drought* is that of the endless 'dune limbo' covering the sea shore, 'a zone of nothingness' (*D.* 119) draining the characters of all sense of time and personal identity. For Ransom and the other inhabitants of Mount Royal, the silence and emptiness of the timeless beaches, 'suspended in an endless interval as flaccid and enduring as the wet dunes themselves' (*D.* 120), can only lead to the gradual erosion of individuality and its submergence by the formless sandy waste.

As Ransom's thoughts become dominated by his struggle for physical survival and his quest for spiritual enlightenment, his interaction with the other characters becomes increasingly functional. This lack of emotional commitment in human relationships (which, in many ways, prefigures Ballard's later theories on the 'death of affect'[3]) is accompanied by the loss of a more general sense of community which, in Ransom's mind, is associated with the death of the river. The role of the river had until then been to establish 'unseen links between the people living on the margins of the channel' (*D.* 13). With the disappearance of 'this great moderator, which cast its bridges between all animate and inanimate objects alike', Ransom concludes, 'each of them would literally be an island in an archipelago drained of time' (*D.* 14). At the end of the closing chapter of the novel, however, Ransom seems to have regained a sense of wholeness and inner reconciliation in the light of which any previous sense of emotional isolation seems almost irrelevant: 'To his surprise, he noticed that he no longer cast any shadow on to the sand, as if he had at last completed his journey across the margins of the inner landscape he had carried in his mind for so many years' (*D.* 188).

One of the 'villains' in the novel is the architect Richard Foster Lomax, whose mind and personality are trapped in obsolete categories of thought and 'formed by his intense focus upon the immediate present' (*D.* 44). Because he remains mentally isolated from the outside world, Lomax fails to grasp the universal implications of the disaster and is described by Ransom as 'the serpent in this dusty Eden . . . trying to grasp back his apple, and preserve intact, if only for a few weeks, the world before the drought' (*D.* 176). Like Strangman in *The Drowned World*, Lomax's self-destructive behaviour is directly linked with his wish to deny or reverse the progress of the catastrophe. Other negative, life-denying powers of a totally different kind are embodied by the sinister and belligerent Reverend Johnstone whose final apocalyptic sermon interprets the drought as a purging force and an answer to 'mankind's unconscious hopes for the end of their present world' (D. 41).

The Crystal World revolves around an African rain forest whose flora and fauna have been transformed into crystal statues. In the course of the narrative, it is discovered that other parts of the world are undergoing the same change which also seems to be affecting the Sun and several distant galaxies. Ballard's novel presents another avatar of the 'Dissolving Hero' in the person of Dr Edward Sanders, a physician specializing in the treatment of leprosy. Typically, the crystallizing process – which also affects human bodies – causes Sanders little worry as he comes to welcome it as part of the natural order of things, a kind of archeopsychic rite of passage leading the animate and inanimate world to 'an ultimate macrocosmic zero beyond the wildest dreams of Plato and Democritus' (CW 96). Whereas Sanders remains moved by an urge to transcend the limits of 'our ordinary lack-lustre world' (CW 94), his friend Suzanne Clair, who has contracted leprosy and later becomes the leader of a colony of black lepers, finds in the deadly beauty and glittering permanence of the crystal forest a means of freeing herself and her followers from the ravages of the disease.

The entropic sites of Ballard's early novels do not seem to evoke any literary equivalents or predecessors. By contrast, the connections between Ballard's visual imagination and the work of Surrealist painters such as Max Ernst, Salvador Dali, Paul Delvaux, Giorgio de Chirico and Yves Tanguy have been repeatedly acknowledged and emphasized by the author himself. As is made explicit by the narrator of *The Drought*, Tanguy's painting *Jours de lenteur* (which lends its title to the closing chapter of the novel), 'with its smooth, pebble-like objects, drained of all associations, suspended on a washed tidal floor' (D. 15) is a direct visual correlative of Ballard's lunar, barren landscapes, in which the mineral often tends to prevail over the biological, the inanimate over the animate. In the context of Ballard's fiction, these images of silent, unthinking permanence are meant to convey the characters' acceptance of a state of ontological isolation and a wish to attain, or return to, a state of inorganic peace symbolized, in both *The Drought* and *The Crystal World*, by a timeless and identity-less mineral world.[4]

By concentrating on inner changes and self-discovery rather than action, on imagery rather than plot, Ballard's novels of catastrophe introduced a whole range of new formal and thematic possibilities into science fiction literature. As we have seen, Ballard's talent for colourful doom visions is related to the unveiling of correspondences between outer and inner land-scapes. More often than not, his characters are simultaneously activating and being activated by changes in their immediate environment. They eventually gain a superior state of awareness beyond the terms set by conventional ways of apprehending and transcending reality, including traditional means of understanding, measuring or simply coping with the passing of time. Whereas Ransom's true goal is to attain 'the only final rest from the persistence of memory [which] would come from his absolution in time' (*D*. 37), Sanders sees the frozen grace of the illuminated forest as the promise of a metastatic growth of a crystalline atom capable of duplicating itself infinitely 'and so fill the entire universe, from which simultaneously all time has expired' (*CW* 96).

The need to escape from the pressure of time is also present in many short stories published in the late 1950s and early 1960s. This, in itself, is far from surprising since Ballard began his career as a professional writer at a time when many science fiction tales – whether published in such innovative magazines as *New Worlds* or in pulp magazines and other more 'main-stream' SF publications – took place in an alternative world in which conventional categories of both time and space appear to be 'out of joint'. This tendency is epitomized in various classic SF subgenres, such as the 'alternate' or 'multiple' worlds narrative or the time travel story which proved very popular with a number of prominent New Wave writers, including Brian Aldiss and Michael Moorcock.[5] Some of Ballard's early works, such as 'The Genteel Assassin' (in which a scientist travels back in time to prevent an assassination attempt which resulted in the death of his young wife and finds himself implicated in the original crime) or 'Escapement', a masterpiece of the 'time-loop' story published as early as 1956, make use of the paradoxes of the 'classical' time travel story in a way that remains within the thematic and formal bounds of the genre. In most cases, however, these temporal disruptions and paradoxes are meant to illustrate man's imprisonment in oppressive categories of thought which are often backed by institutionalized forms of public control.

'Concentration City' (originally titled 'Build-Up') portrays an overpopulated city made up of thousands of interrelated levels and sectors in which organized gangs of pyromaniac outcasts engage in a constant battle with the fire police. Refusing to accept the official theory according to which the city extends indefinitely in all directions and thereby leaves him no possibility of escape, M., the protagonist, decides to build a flying machine and leave the city in search of free space. After travelling for several weeks to the furthest reaches of the city, M. realizes that a built-in feature of the megalopolis – combined with the effects of some mysterious spatiotemporal curvature – has trapped him in both time and space, causing him to come back to where and when he started. Whereas 'Chronopolis' centres upon the idea of time as related to psychological coercion and actual political oppression (as exemplified in the hero's rebellion against 'Time Laws' that prohibit the measurement of time), Charles Gifford, the main character of 'The Delta at Sunset', embodies the possibility of resistance against an 'obsessive time-consciousness' (*TB* 118) which undermines his craving for absolute (self-)transcendence. Implied in many of these stories of imprisonment in time and space is a conception of the human condition as that of being trapped in various kinds of psychological, cultural or social confinement. The stories which fall into the interior 'captivity narrative' category, like 'Concentration City' and 'The Delta at Sunset', often involve isolated individuals at odds with societal apparatuses which deny their basic unconscious urges.

'Mr. F. is Mr. F.' and 'Time of Passage', two other early stories centred on temporal disruptions, elaborate significantly more playful modulations on the pattern of psychological and biological devolution discussed above in relation to *The Drowned World*. In the first story, Freeman, a married man in his early forties, begins a process of irremediable physical rejuvenation almost immediately after his wife's pregnancy has been confirmed. Freeman reaches the ultimate stage of his uncanny transformation – which his wife seems to accept as 'a natural concomitant of her own pregnancy' (*DA* 115) and an external projection of her own unborn child – as he eventually returns to the 'drowned world of his childhood' before coming to 'his true beginning, the moment of his conception coinciding with the moment of his extinction, the end of his last birth with the beginning of his first death' (*DA* 120, 121). 'Time of Passage' – whose straight-faced seriousness and absurdist logic is reminiscent of the best stories of Nikolai Gogol – is a hilarious 'inverted' life story told in slow rewind from the day of the protagonist's burial to his birth and beyond. After resurrecting from his grave, a man named Falkman goes backwards through the main stages of his life. He becomes the chairman of several charitable organizations and a prominent member of the business community before entering a phase of deep dejection due to the oncoming death of his future wife, Marion. After her death and resurrection, Falkman becomes a devoted husband and they live happily for a number of years until Marion inexplicably decides to go to live with her parents. Later, Falkman gives up his job and goes to live at his parents' house, an environment which proves rather uncomfortable as his father becomes increasingly critical of him for leaving his job and 'beg[ins] to dominate Falkman, restricting his freedom and reducing his pocket money, even warning him not to play with certain of his friends' (*VH* 81). The story ends with Falkman's ultimate dissolution due to his mother's inverted pregnancy and the prospect of his parents' imminent separation.

'Now: Zero', a playful, metafictional piece biting its own tail and ultimately resulting in the death . . . of the reader, is another successful example of Ballard's use of black humour. Other, more serious, variations on the theme of time-consciousness include 'The Garden of Time', an unusually poetic tale in which a villa inhabited by a couple of sophisticated aristocrats, Count Axel and his wife, is threatened and eventually overrun by a brutal and savage human tide. 'The Time Tombs' tells of grave robbers who seek out the holographic molecular transcriptions of an ancient civilization, selling their precious loot to the 'Psycho-History Museums'. 'The Day of Forever', which remains one of Ballard's most compelling works to date, takes place

15

against the background of a no-longer-revolving earth in the North African sector of Columbine Sept Heures, an area marooned in an endless dusk. One of Ballard's most visual stories, 'The Day of Forever' is filled with references to the Surrealist paintings of Max Ernst, Giorgio de Chirico and Paul Delvaux, whose work also makes a cameo appearance in *The Drowned World*. One of these paintings, Delvaux's *The Echo* – which depicts a naked Junoesque woman walking among immaculate ruins under a midnight sky (*DF* 9) – is of particular importance as it reminds Halliday, the central character or 'consciousness' of the story, of one of his recurrent dreams. Halliday eventually meets a mysterious dark-haired and pale-faced woman named Gabrielle Szabo, whom he recognizes as the 'dark lamia of all his dreams' (*DF* 15). Ballard's obsession with the effects of time on the individual consciousness once again predominates when Halliday, watching Gabrielle Szabo walking among the ruins of the Roman city of Leptis Magna, realizes that 'the moonlit phantoms of his mind [move] freely between the inner and outer landscapes' (*DF* 20), thereby reasserting Ballard's view of human beings as conditioned and motivated by their physical environment.

In the much admired and discussed 'The Voices of Time', perhaps Ballard's most significant short work of fiction written in the early 1960s, some of the major themes discussed so far acquire an even more universal and, indeed, cosmic signifi-cance. Like Ballard's early novels, 'The Voices of Time' does away with the traumatic effects and anxiety-laden atmosphere of the traditional disaster tale. The story deals with nothing less than the agony of the entire universe, a process of cosmic exhaustion allegedly caused by heavier radiation levels emitted by a cooling sun. Starting from the hypothesis that increasingly high levels of radiation can reactivate two dormant and apparently useless genes which occur in all living organisms, a scientist named Whitby decides to irradiate the 'silent genes' which, once deciphered, would deliver a 'divine message' about the future of mankind. Whitby's experiment, however, proves a complete failure whose horrifying implications (the organisms he has irradiated, far from providing a remedy, enter 'a final phase of totally disorganized growth') lead him to commit suicide. Meanwhile, numerical signals from the Canes Venatici sector have started to send a countdown whose end will coincide with the end of the cosmos. The other central characters are Dr Powers, who has become subject to narcoma (a sleeping sickness related to the silent genes which, in the long run, causes humans to lapse into a permanent, dreamless sleep), his girlfriend, Coma, and a man named Kaldren whom Powers has surgically narcotomized, removing his capacity to fall asleep.[6] The rest of the story is about Powers's attempts to free himself from the effects of the narcoma syndrome, as well as from the approaching death of the universe, by building an immense mandala in the desert. Having irradiated his own silent genes, Powers positions himself at the centre of the mandala and, hearing 'a thousand voices that together told of the total time elapsed in the life of the escarpment', becomes aware of the 'enormous age' of the landscape that surrounds him.

The basic idea of 'The Voices of Time' is emblematic of Ballard's attempt to create what Sartre, commenting on the fiction of William Faulkner (a writer with whom Ballard also shares an obsession with flight), once called 'a metaphysics of time'.[7] Implicit in this attempt is a Bergsonian notion that the inner rhythms of mental life cannot be contained within the linearity of man-made instruments of time measurement such as clocks and watches. (Significantly, Powers throws away his alarm clock and wristwatch before embarking on his spiritual quest.) Ballard's story, however, does not really adopt Bergson's notion of time as 'pure duration', which still relied on the existence of a quintessential form of memory fusing the totality of our past and present experiences. It argues, instead, for a more radical deliverance from all temporal anxieties which can only be achieved through death. Indeed, it is only by letting his body dissolve into the cosmos that Powers manages at last to envision the stream of universal time before 'melting into the vast continuum of the current, which bore him out into the centre of the great channel, sweeping him onward beyond hope but at last at rest, down the broadening reaches of the river of eternity' (*VT* 40).

The principle of global dissipation, the decline of cosmic energy and the ensuing annihilation of organic life which constitute the premises of 'The Voices of Time' point in the direction of entropy, a scientific notion frequently used – both literally and metaphorically – by many New Wave writers. The principle of entropy originally refers to the measure of the energy that is not available for work in a thermodynamic process. More importantly, at least in the context of Ballard's work, its cosmological extension designates a hypothetical tendency of the universe to attain a state of maximum homogeneity in which all matter is at a uniform temperature and eventually brings about the 'heat death' of the universe. Ballard's concern with entropy allies him not only with other representatives of the British New Wave but also with a whole line of post-war novelists (many of them American) whose work displays an equally consistent vision of the universe as regressing to a state of absolute uniformity and inertness.[8] Interestingly enough, 'The Voices of Time' was published in the same year as Thomas Pynchon's short story 'Entropy', in which a man named Callisto locks himself up in his apartment which he decides to transform into 'a tiny enclave of regularity in the city's chaos, alien to the vagaries of the weather, national politics, of any civil disorder'.[9] While meditating upon the significance of his own efforts to ward off the material and spiritual disorder of the outside world, the protagonist of Pynchon's story finds in the second law of thermodynamics 'an adequate metaphor to apply to certain phenomena in his own world' and discovers in the phenomenon of American consumerism 'a similar tendency from the least to the most probable, from differentiation to sameness, from ordered individuality to a kind of chaos'.[10] If 'The Voices of Time' seems completely devoid of the specific social and political subtext of 'Entropy', Ballard's use of the entropy metaphor nonetheless shares Pynchon's vision of human life releasing energy at an accelerating rate and ready to succumb to a form of emotional and intellectual 'heat-death'. While Pynchon applies the entropy metaphor to the workings of society as a whole, Ballard is primarily concerned with the decline of vital energy within the human consciousness itself.

Together with a recurrent interest in the dialectics of time and space, the common denominator of Ballard's early works is an attempt to expand traditional science fiction plots and themes by merging the outer world of reality and the hidden life of the psyche – a method Ballard himself was to term 'inner space' poetics (*UGM* 84). As a result, the central conflict of Ballard's stories is more often the result of internal changes (many of which, as we have seen, are motivated by a sense of inexorable loss and decay) occurring within the mind of the protagonist than of confrontation between people. Most of the characters who people his early novels and short stories are therefore not fully-fledged individuals. Rather, they stand for a specific abstraction or obsession which threatens to destabilize their sense of self and prompts them to invent their own 'reality' in order to adjust to their new environment.[11] In 'Minus One', a story contained in the collection, *The Disaster Area*, this blurring of boundaries between reality and illusion is applied not to the workings of consciousness itself but to a specific social environment. The story takes place at Green Hill Asylum, a mental hospital which the narrator describes as 'one of those institutions which are patronized by the wealthier members of the community and in effect serve the role of private prisons' (*DA* 95). A man named James Hinton succeeds in becoming the first patient ever to escape from the asylum. Since public exposure of the incident would ruin the reputation of Green Hill as a maximum security hospital as well as his own career, Dr Mellinger, the director of the asylum, decides against notifying the civil authorities of Hinton's escape. Instead, he succeeds in convincing his colleagues that Hinton never actually existed and was in fact simply the result of 'a concatenation of errors' (*DA* 101) which eventually led them to '[invest] an entirely non-existent individual with the fictions of personality' (*DA* 98). The story ends with the unexpected appearance of Mrs Hinton, who, having come to visit her husband, is diagnosed as suffering from terrible delusions and immediately confined to the asylum.

That this story of deceit and exclusion takes place in a mental institution is, of course, no coincidence. As will become clear in the following chapters of this study, 'Minus One' prefigures Ballard's ongoing interest not just in the relationship between the real and the imaginary but also in the dialectics of deviance and normalcy, a concern which aligns his work, at least to some extent, with the theories of R. D. Laing and other representatives of the anti-psychiatric school.[12] What emerges from Ballard's story is indeed a conception of deviance as defined –

19

and even engendered – by an institution governed by exclusion, regulation and personal ambition.

Characteristically, the James Hinton case represents, in Dr Mellinger's mind, 'more than a simple problem of breached security' – it is 'a symbol of something grievously at fault with the very foundations of Green Hill' (*DA* 95), a reality Mellinger is to deny for fear of undermining the true vocation of the hospital, which is to confine individuals whose presence would otherwise be embarrassing to their relatives or to society as a whole. On a more strategic level, 'Minus One' can thus be read as an allegorical demonstration of how the survival of certain social structures is necessarily guaranteed by various principles of illusion and repression, including the shutting out of whatever threatens to upset the basic set of beliefs on which they are founded.

Another early short story, 'The Insane Ones', offers a rather more equivocal and satirical extrapolation from official attitudes taken towards madness. The story is concerned with the enforcement by an ultra-conservative government of a 'Mental Freedom' law whose main purpose is to '[enshrine] the individual's freedom to be insane' and outlaw 'all forms of psychic control, from the innocent market survey to lobotomy' (*DF* 117). The profession of psychiatry, in particular, comes under fierce attack as an agent of social chaos and 'an encouragement to weakness and lack of will' (*DF* 121). As for the psychotics themselves, they are allowed to wander where they want and gradually become the sacred cows of a community succumbing to a peculiar form of collective paranoia. Clearly, the 'lesson' to be drawn from 'The Insane Ones' is not merely that the frontier between rationality and insanity is hard to establish. Rather, the story is significant for its suggestion that the establishment of such a (semi-)totalitarian state depends on the creation of a collective fiction and the search for a scapegoat on whom to discharge a variety of private and public anxieties. Ironically, the repressive measures implemented by the state police – which 'had begun as a popular reaction against "subliminal living" and the uncontrolled extension of techniques of mass manipulation for political and economic ends' such as are described in 'The Subliminal Man' (see discussion below, chapter 2) – are originally taken in the name of the absolute freedom and self-determination of the individual.

With its Swiftian sardonicisms and disquieting black humour, 'The Insane Ones' ranks among Ballard's most accomplished short stories. Its treatment of the problematic division between the freedom of unreason and the deadening effects of 'subliminal living' (*DF* 117) – combined as it is with a dystopian analysis of the repressive function of the state apparatus – also makes it a creative and satirical counterpart to the theories Michel Foucault had just started to develop when Ballard's story was published in the significantly less academic context of the science fiction magazine *Amazing Stories*. Unlike Foucault's *Madness and Civilization* (1961), whose purpose was to comment on Western society's exclusion of madness in the name of various kinds of social hygiene and moral uniformity, Ballard's 'The Insane Ones' is an indictment of how certain modern avatars of public welfare and enlightened legislation could lead to even tighter forms of social and psychological control.

3

The Death of Affect

Most of Ballard's readers would probably agree that his fiction as a whole, despite its apparently antithetical directions, is a coherent and consistent literary achievement; one in which the same obsessions recur over and over again under different forms and in different contexts. *The Kindness of Women* (1991) – Ballard's brilliant, and largely underestimated, sequel to *Empire of the Sun* – appears in many ways as a kind of link between the different 'parallel careers' which make up his oeuvre. His retrospective account of the 'craze years' of the 1960s, in particular, contains a number of semi-autobiographical keys to the interpretation of the major themes and motifs of his work and to what he himself calls his 'library of extreme metaphors'. Describing the 'unique alchemy of the imagination' taking place in the 1960s, Ballard sees the new media landscape then emerging as 'a laboratory designed specifically to cure [him] of all [his] obsessions'. 'The brutalizing newsreels of civil wars and assassinations, the stylization of televised violence into an anthology of design statements', he goes on, 'were matched by a pornography of science that took its material, not from nature, but from the deviant curiosity of the scientist' (*KW* 185).

Such were the specific methodological premises of *The Atrocity Exhibition* (1970), Ballard's first foray into the kind of avant-gardist experimentalism which earned him a cult-reputation as a 'far-out' writer. The volume contains fifteen 'chapters' or 'condensed novels' ranging from four to fifteen pages. Each of them contains a series of interrelated vignettes gravitating around the psychopathological states of a central figure, that of a psychiatrist suffering from a nervous breakdown, variously named Travis, Talbot, Traven, Tallis, Trabert, Talbert, and Travers. As Ballard himself comments, the protagonist of the collection is a kind of portmanteau entity 'appear[ing] in a succession of roles, ranging across a spectrum of possibilities available to each of us in our interior lives' (*AE* 91).

An important aspect of the British New Wave school (which also characterized, for instance, Michael Moorcock's famous Jerry Cornelius stories), the exploded structure of the episodes is reminiscent of the famous 'cut-up' writing technique of William S. Burroughs and Brion Gysin.[1] But Ballard's 'condensed novels' are experimental not only because they leave out such standard novelistic elements as plot, normal relations of time and place and conventional characterization, but also because they are literally organized in the mode of a scientific experiment. Presenting its subjects with a detached attitude and an almost medical frankness about their movements, activities and psychosexual idiosyncrasies, Ballard's *Atrocity Exhibition* treats its characters less like psychologically significant individuals and more like laboratory data to be analysed in the context of the author's investigation of 'the unique vocabulary and grammar of late 20th century life' (*AE* 87). From amidst the welter of fantasies and imaginary scenarios developed in Ballard's narrative, 'the safe and sane voice' (*AE* 59) of Dr Nathan, who conducts most of the experiments related in the collection, emerges as the last repository of scientific objectivity. The cold, imperturbable stance of the psychiatrist's reports – which attempt to track specific psychological processes through an examination of the patients' physical functioning and external behaviour – is largely responsible for the conceptual continuity of Ballard's collages. Throughout the collection, Nathan remains strangely distant both from the repeated atrocities and lethal scenarios that gravitate around the insane mind of the book's protagonist, and from the psychopathological fantasies of the other mental patients confined to his asylum, whose deeper motives he is to investigate and elucidate in such a technical and systematic fashion.

One immediate effect of Ballard's clinical approach is that it pre-empts any form of complicity or empathy on the part of the reader, who will find it all the more difficult to identify with any of the characters since some of them die at the end of an episode only to re-emerge, in a typically New Wave manner, in a later section. By eradicating all inflections of subjectivity from his narrative, Ballard seems to be seeking a Barthesian 'degree zero' of writing which had already been adumbrated in the anxiety-free psychological landscapes of his early novels and short stories. Ballard's style – which is consistently blank, neutral and stripped of all the conventional artifices of fiction – bears an interesting relation to the 'objective style' of Alain Robbe-Grillet's 'new novels', which also share with Ballard's *Atrocity Exhibition* a conception of narrative as a sequence of primarily visual perceptions, an ability to sustain the dispassionate gaze of the scientist and, as we shall see, a fascination with objects and human beings that exist above all in a closed relation to themselves, to the detriment of the metaphoric and symbolic aura of traditional, 'humanist' fiction.

More often than not, the psychopathological landscapes depicted in *The Atrocity Exhibition* convey the erosion of human relationships and the individual self into a state of two-dimensional anonymity. This particular aspect of the collection can largely be accounted for by Ballard's interest in the pop art of Andy Warhol, Robert Rauschenberg and, most notably, Tom Wesselman, whose series of paintings *The Great American Nude* becomes the conceptual core of the sixth section of the collection. Ballard's indebtedness to Wesselman is linked with his rejection of the metaphysical 'depth' of traditional art and of its accompanying tendency to represent the subject as a unified, self-present whole. In Wesselman's paintings, he writes, 'the bland surface defuses the subject' (*AE* 55), reducing it to an abstract, flat silhouette from which every mark of human presence fades. Likewise, Ballard's *Atrocity Exhibition* – in which language and the self constantly seem on the verge of becoming engulfed in the claustrophobic angles and curves of the subject's architectural environment – explores the consciousnesses of human beings who tend to surrender to the world of objects and even tend to 'become mere extensions of the geometries of situations' (*AE* 87). They are subsequently neutralized into a space beyond good and evil which reflects the latent desire of the postmodern consciousness to achieve, at least at a metaphorical level, 'the total fusion and nondifferentiation of all matter' (*AE* 33):

Murder. Tallis stood behind the door of the lounge, shielded from the sunlight on the balcony, and considered the white cube of the room. At intervals Karen Novotny moved across it, carrying out a sequence of apparently random acts. Already she was confusing the perspectives of the room, transforming it into a dislocated clock. She noticed Tallis behind the door and walked towards him. Tallis waited for her to leave. Her figure interrupted the junction between the walls in the corner on his right. After a few seconds her presence became an unbearable intrusion into the time geometry of the room. (*AE* 43)

This excerpt is characteristic of Ballard's ability to defamiliar-ize our everyday environment and explore the junctions between bodily and objective geometries, as well as the boundaries between the organic and the nonorganic. On a superficial level, the problematic of time and space which inform Ballard's *Atrocity Exhibition* can thus be seen as a continuation of the basic entropic landscapes described in some of his early works. Perhaps more importantly, however, it is also a reflection of Ballard's ongoing fascination with Surrealist painting and its capacity to produce 'a heightened or alternate reality beyond that familiar to our sight or senses' (*UGM* 84). The discovery of this dialectic between psychological and external realities bears striking similarities with a principle of Surrealist art Ballard defines as a 'calculated submission of the impulses and fantasies of our inner lives to the rigours of time and space' (*UGM* 84). The 'continuous present' in which most of Ballard's characters evolve echoes the author's own interpretation of the manne-quin-like figures in Giorgio de Chirico's painting *The Disquieting Muses* as 'human beings from whom all time has been eroded, and reduced to the essence of their own geometries' (*UGM* 86).[2] The 'redemptive and therapeutic power' Ballard associates with the Surrealists' inner space poetics, however, seems absent from the neurological nightmares of *The Atrocity Exhibition*. As indicated by the section reproduced above, Ballard's vignettes often seem to exist in a sterilized vacuum which seems quite remote from the deep, 'archeopsychic' sense of self experienced by the protagonists of his disaster novels. As in Wesselman's depthless nudes and much of Pop art, what remains here is an unsubstantial, reified 'I' lost in a maze of fractured images and phantasmagoric fictions which culminate in the assassination fantasies entertained by Ballard's patients, whose virtual victims range from Marilyn Monroe and Brigitte Bardot to Soong Mayling (a.k.a. Madame Chiang Kai-Shek), Jacqueline Kennedy or Princess Margaret.

And indeed, Ballard's *Atrocity Exhibition* – for all its abstract, and often rather obscure, logic – is firmly rooted in its historical background. One of its main goals is to study the subliminal effects of iconic media events – such as the Vietnam war, the assassination of John Fitzgerald Kennedy, or the suicide of Marilyn Monroe – on the contemporary mind. Ballard's preoccupation with the mass media and the possibility that the new technological landscape may trigger unconscious drives is central to the grammar of pornography and violence that runs through the whole collection. Commenting on the goals and methods of his 'condensed novels', Ballard
argues that their true subject matter is 'the irrational violence of modern society', which he sees as resulting from 'the commu- nications explosion of the '60s'[3] in which 'real violence, frequently life, as it occurs, becomes part of a huge entertain- ments industry' (*R/S* 154). The Vietnam war, for instance, is described, in the section entitled 'Love and Napalm: Export U.S.A.', as 'a limited military confrontation with strong audience participation via TV and news media, satisfying low-threshold fantasies of violence and aggression' (*AE* 105), the 'latent sexuality' of which is effectively mediated by a number of important figures from the interconnected worlds of politics and show-business. Numerous other pieces contained in the collection – such as the infamous 'Why I Want to Fuck Ronald Reagan' – expose the transformation of violence into an easily consumable commodity by media whose main function is to apprehend and manipulate external reality on our behalf. The thermodynamic principle of entropy, briefly discussed in the opening chapter of this study as a model for the emotional and intellectual 'heat-death' of the individual mind, becomes here an adequate metaphor for the progressive standardization of world consciousness in the mass-media age; the dark side, so to speak, of the instant communicational networks of the Global Access utopia. Lastly, the definition of 'entropy' used, by analogy, in information and data transmission technology ('a measure of the loss of information in a transmitted signal or message') also applies to the dynamics of Ballard's book, in that

it insists on the kind of 'devalued' reality and the ensuing dissolution of any solid basis for moral and political discernment brought about by the uncritical 'dispersal' of information in the mass-media age.

Ballard's numerous annotations to the new, revised edition of his book further emphasize the analytical strain of his 'condensed novels'. While confirming his intention to decode the subliminal meaning and 'hidden agendas' (*AE* 80) of our everyday lives, they also acknowledge the importance of Freud's classic distinction between the latent and the manifest content of the subconscious mind which, Ballard argues, should now be applied to the 'outer world' (*AE* 111) of a reality increasingly dominated by an endless, metastatic flow of free-floating images and signs. To the paratactic logic of media manipulation, Ballard thus opposes his own particular brand of semiotic analysis. Because the contemporary world as mediated by modern communication technology appears as a concatenation of seemingly unrelated signifiers, Ballard has to resort to a medium whose narrative structure is itself nonlinear and associational.

Automobiles, highways, advertising billboards, TV newsreels, movie stars, contemporary urban architecture, political glamour, nuclear armament, chemical plants, suburb culture – all are interpreted as symptomatic of the psychosexual significance of our daily lives in the late twentieth century. As was the case in his earlier novels and short stories, these external landscapes appear as direct equivalents of the inner world of the psyche. Ballard therefore emerges less as a 'fiction' writer than as a secular exegete of the emotional and spiritual drought of post-industrial Western culture. His self-appointed task is to disclose a number of meaningful correspondences between various aspects of our private and collective experiences. In this respect, also, Ballard's fictional experiments resemble the paintings and collages of the mental patients in Dr Nathan's hospital who, 'with their fusion of Eniwetok and Luna Park, Freud and Elizabeth Taylor', evoke 'insoluble dreams' (*AE* 1) to which no single frame of interpretation can do justice. In fact, the insanity of Ballard's patients, far from being due to their failure to make contact with the outside world, results from an *excess* of awareness which makes it impossible for them to cope with what Dr Nathan calls 'the phenomenology of the universe, the specific and independent existence of separate objects and events, however trivial and inoffensive these may seem': 'A spoon, for example, offends [Traven] by the mere fact of its existence in time and space. More than this, one could say that the precise, if largely random, configuration of atoms in the universe at any given moment, one never again to be repeated, seems to him to be preposterous by virtue of its unique identity...' (AE 33). According to Nathan's report – which implicitly draws upon a number of principles enunciated by modern physics, including Heisenberg's uncertainty principle – the patients' endeavours to make sense of a reality in a constant state of flux accounts for their obsession with the new, multiple levels of meaning offered by their physical environment.

In the following passage, Nathan interprets Travis's 'extreme sensitivity to the volumes and geometry of the world around him, and their immediate translation into psychological terms' as the reflection of 'a belated attempt to return to a symmetrical world' (AE 8). Nathan's comments on Travis's quest for pre-embryonic, symmetrical analogies remind us of Ballard's earlier stories of devolution. They also add another, more affirmative dimension to his patient's fantasies, one which points forward to his later awareness that 'the rectilinear forms of his conscious reality were warped elements from some placid and harmonious future' (AE 18):

> **The Lost Symmetry of the Blastosphere**. 'This reluctance to accept the fact of his own consciousness, ' Dr Nathan wrote, 'may reflect certain positional difficulties in the immediate context of time and space. The right-angle spiral of a stairwell may remind him of similar biases within the chemistry of the biological kingdom. This can be carried to remarkable lengths – for example, the jutting balconies of the Hilton Hotel have become identified with the lost gill-slits of the dying film actress, Elizabeth Taylor. Much of Travis's thought' concerns what he terms "the lost symmetry of the blastosphere" – the primitive precursor of the embryo that is the last structure to preserve perfect symmetry in all planes. It occurred to Travis that our own bodies may conceal the rudiments of a symmetry not only about the vertical axis but also the horizontal. One recalls Goethe's notion that the skull is formed of modified vertebrae – similarly, the bones of the pelvis may constitute the remains of a lost sacral skull.' (AE 7–8)

Ballard's blurring of accepted distinctions between normality and deviance (which is further reinforced by the ambiguous position of his central protagonist, who combines the roles of patient and psychiatrist) echoes the author's own comments on William S. Burroughs's novel, *The Naked Lunch*, and its comparison of organized society 'with that of its most extreme opposite, the invisible society of drug addicts'. Burroughs's conclusion, Ballard writes, is that 'the two are not very different, certainly at the points where they make the closest contacts – in prisons and psychiatric institutions' (*UGM* 127–8). In many ways, the narrative and cultural function of the two-dimensional characters of *The Atrocity Exhibition* strongly resembles what Ballard himself calls the 'metaphorical' value of Burroughs's own sadistic scientists and heroin-addicted perverts whose deranged psyches often appear as direct extensions of the death-oriented logic of outside circumstances.

In this respect, Ballard's proposition that 'sexual intercourse can no longer be regarded as a personal and isolated activity, but is seen to be a vector in a public complex involving automobile styling, politics and mass communications' points to 'the nonsexual roots of sexuality' (*AE*, pp. 104, vii) which Burroughs himself sees as the real subject of *The Atrocity Exhibition*. The section entitled 'Why I Want to Fuck Ronald Reagan' is perhaps the ultimate example of Ballard's interest in decoding the covert libidinal strategies at work in the technological landscape. Ballard's piece – which prompted Doubleday to destroy the first American edition of *The Atrocity Exhibition* – reports the results of studies conducted upon patients in terminal paresis. The subjects of the tests are required to devise a series of simulated auto-crashes resulting in the death of the then newly appointed governor of California. The ultimate goal of the experiment is to define 'the auto-disaster of maximized audience arousal' on the basis of Reagan's 'optimum sex-death' (*AE* 119, 122). Clearly, Ballard's purpose here is not to invite the reader to partake in the patients' sexual fantasies, nor is it to suggest that car crashes are inherently pleasant or sexy experiences. The main target of Ballard's critique is of course the media culture itself and its tendency to trivialize cruelty and package violence into a commercial product. Ironically, the figure of Ronald Reagan is the perfect illustration of the duplicity of the media image.

Building on the contradiction between his affable rhetoric and slick body language, on the one hand, and the aggressiveness of his right-wing politics, on the other, Reagan's enormous and universal impact as a media emblem epitomizes what Ballard denounced elsewhere as 'politics conducted as a branch of advertising' (*R/S* 97). Similar strategies of *détournement* of famous media figures are deployed in 'You: Coma: Marilyn Monroe' (in which Tallis attempts to make sense of the film star's tragic death by dismembering and reshaping her mind and body in terms of the 'time geometry' of desert dunes) and 'The Assassination of John Fitzgerald Kennedy Considered as a Downhill Motor Race', which was inspired by Alfred Jarry's farcical piece, 'The Crucifixion Considered as an Uphill Bicycle Race'.

Some readers and critics have found the amoral (or perhaps one should say post-moral) quality of Ballard's *Atrocity Exhibition* problematic, in that it often appears as a symptom of, rather than an alternative to, what the author sees as the present age's loss of social and moral commitment. Others have been shocked by the crude violence and the sexual explicitness of Ballard's stories. One could object to such criticism that Ballard never tries to impose his reality onto the reader but is merely offering us his own interpretation of late-twentieth-century consciousness. The same objection applies to his tendency to dwell on images of atrocities, mutilations and gratuitous violence. In this respect, one has to admit that the geometrical stylization of violence which prevails in many of Ballard's novels never leads to its subsequent aestheticization: what Ballard is concerned with is the secret 'nightmare logic' of contemporary violence, not its glamour or commercial appeal. Ballard is therefore neither a moralist nor an apologist, but a visionary observer of what he perceives as the cold post-morality of a fragmented, narcissistic age.

For Ballard, the gradual numbing of our emotional responses to mediatized violence has led to various forms of physical and mental alienation, including a phenomenon the author memorably called the 'death of affect' (*AE* 77, *R/S* 96). As Ballard recently suggested in *The Kindness of Women*, our gradual alienation from any kind of direct (that is, unmediated) response to experience – combined with the unlimited expansion of the mind's possibilities afforded to us by modern technology – has left us 'free to pursue our own psychopathologies as a game' (*KW* 221). The radical existential freedom thus acquired by Ballard's characters makes them increasingly attracted to perversions. Still, the images of sexual perversion which abound in Ballard's *Atrocity Exhibition* and *Crash* (which he called the first 'technological' porn novel) are almost entirely deprived of erotic content, as they are always depicted in strictly technical terms. The aseptic abstractness of Ballard's vignettes is best understood in the light of Dr Nathan's remark, in 'The Assassination Weapon', that 'science is the ultimate pornography, analytic activity whose main aim is to isolate objects or events from their contexts in time and space' (*AE* 36). More generally, Ballard's fiction depicts a fin-de-siècle atmosphere in which perversions, which often stand for the stylization and the conceptualization of pleasure, have become the last possibility of attaining any form of sexual or psychological gratification.

In the light of these ideas we might consider again the enormous impact of Surrealist art on Ballard's anti-narratives. The work of Salvador Dali, in particular, contains some of the basic ingredients of Ballard's *Atrocity Exhibition*, including the simulation of mental diseases, an interest in the double significance of things, the reshaping of the body by its immersion in the perverse eroticism of the unconscious, a nostalgia for a lost state of pre-uterine peacefulness, as well as the reliance on paranoia and other interpretative disorders as a critical method. Dali was also one of the first modern artists to incorporate and reflect on the psychosexual function of such mass-media figures as Shirley Temple and Mae West, the latter of whom makes a memorable appearance in the closing section of Ballard's book. The work of German-born Surrealist artist Hans Bellmer appears as another important influence on Ballard's treatment of the body in *The Atrocity Exhibition*. The menacing obscenity of Bellmer's articulated doll sculptures, which are briefly mentioned in the section devoted to Wesselman's *The Great American Nude*, anticipate the fractured profiles and magnified details of body parts that people Ballard's collection. Bellmer's 'interanatomic dreams', as well as his notion of the 'physical unconscious' – which referred to the artist's capacity to create hybrid bodies by fusing conflicting attitudes and movements into a single image – seems particularly apt in the context of Ballard's own attempts to give expression to the paradoxical anatomy of the unconscious. Lastly, Ballard's own experience, as a medical student at Cambridge, of the practice of dissection as 'an eye-opener' and 'a tremendous experience in the lack of integrity of the flesh' (R/S 157) is also especially relevant here.

As Ballard himself points out, another notable antecedent of his preoccupation with the dialectics of body and landscape was that of the French physiologist Étienne Jules Marey, who produced a series of multiple-exposure photographs or 'chronograms' depicting 'the moving figure of a man represented as a series of dune-like humps' (UGM 85). Marey's chronophotographic technique makes an intriguing appearance in the opening section of The Atrocity Exhibition. Marey's chronograms, which Dr Nathan describes as 'multiple-exposure photographs in which the element of time is visible', emerge as an interesting correlative to Travis's own collection of photographs which, when arranged in a series, cause 'the familiar surroundings of our lives, even our smallest gestures . . . to have totally altered meanings' (AE 5).

The following passage, in which Tallis equates the physical aspect of his lover, Karen Novotny, with the dune landscape around her, is a typical illustration of how the central consciousness of Ballard's book seeks to disrupt conventional relationships of space and time and create a speculative method that performs the 'marriage of Freud and Euclid' (AE 86). Tallis's attempts to eroticize the landscape, which lead indirectly to the gradual consumption of the woman's identity in the eyes of her beholder, is also characteristic:

> **The Persistence of the Beach**. The white flanks of the dunes reminded him of the endless promenades of Karen Novotny's body – diorama of flesh and hillock; the broad avenues of the thighs, piazzas of pelvis and abdomen, the closed arcades of the womb. This terracing of Karen's body in the landscape of the beach in some way diminished the identity of the young woman asleep in her apartment. He walked among the displaced contours of her pectoral girdle. What time could be read off the slopes and inclines of this inorganic musculature, the drifting planes of its face? (AE 43)

The analytical and technological aridity of Ballard's Atrocity

Exhibition, added to the compression and obliquities of the narrative itself, is such that the collection somehow gains from a discontinuous reading. Read one after another, Ballard's sex- and technology-obsessed fantasies indeed run the risk of straining the patience of even the most dedicated reader. Despite, and perhaps because of, its obsessive and repetitive overtones, however, Ballard's collection shows a remarkable grasp of political as well as psychological possibilities. The painstaking exactness of Ballard's style, and the strange poetry that emerges from his rendering of the perverse and paranoid neuroses of the contemporary mind, make it one of the most disquieting, but also one of the most accomplished, experimental works of modern fiction.

4

An Alphabet of Wounds

Crash (1973) was directly inspired by an homonymous 'condensed novel' of *The Atrocity Exhibition* and, in many ways, appears as a linearized, and more accessible, sequel to what was until then Ballard's most radically experimental work. The story takes place in contemporary London. A narrator named James Ballard reports on how his own automobile crash – in which a passenger from the other car is fatally injured – triggers in him a number of compelling obsessions, all of which gravitate around the 'perverse eroticism of the car-crash, as painful as the drawing of an exposed organ through the aperture of a surgical wound' (C. 17). As Ballard becomes aware of his new state of consciousness, he also becomes increasingly unsatisfied with his familiar concrete and emotional surroundings. His relationship with his wife, in particular, has become 'almost totally abstracted, maintained by a series of imaginary games and perversities' (C. 83). Most prominent among these is the daily ritual of describing to each other their recent and future infidelities while having sexual intercourse. These vicarious fantasies, however, soon prove unsatisfying after the accident has shattered Ballard's previous sense of self and become a catalyst for the emergence of a number of as-yet unimagined pleasures that would give a new meaning to his blunted personality and transcend 'all the hopes and fancies of [his] suburban enclave, drenched in a thousand infidelities' (C. 49).

> The crash was the only experience I had been through for years. For the first time I was in physical confrontation with my own body, an inexhaustible encyclopedia of pains and discharges, with the hostile gaze of other people, and with the fact of the dead man. After being bombarded endlessly with road-safety-propaganda it was almost a relief to find myself in an actual accident. Like everyone else

bludgeoned by these billboard harangues and television films of imaginary accidents, I had felt a vague sense of unease that the gruesome climax of my life was being rehearsed years in advance, and would take place on some highway or road junction known only to the makers of these films. At times I had even speculated on the kind of traffic accident in which I would die. (C. 39)

What emerges from the 'brothel of images' that henceforth dominates Ballard's mind is an emphasis on the cerebral dimension of desire which enables him to bring himself to orgasm simply by thinking of the car in which he and his lover Dr Helen Remington (the wife of the man killed in the accident) '[perform] their sexual acts' (C. 83). The other characters of the story, including Mrs Catherine Ballard and Dr Helen Remington, undergo similar psychological changes reflected in their subsequent techno-porn affairs with Ballard, most of which take place in cars, along the motorway. Later, Ballard encounters Vaughan, a deranged scientist who further initiates the narrator into 'the mould of sexual possibilities yet to be created in a hundred experimental car-crashes' (C. 177). Vaughan's fascination with crashes and their mysterious erotic implications eventually leads him to crave, and nearly achieve, a self-immolating car-crash union with movie star Elizabeth Taylor that echoes a number of similar simulated fantasies in *The Atrocity Exhibition*. Ballard's sense of an oncoming, well-rehearsed choreography of interrelated crashes is confirmed by the death of Seagrave (a stuntman at the Shepperton film studios who becomes one of Vaughan's most dedicated followers), who kills himself in a car accident, wearing Elizabeth Taylor's wig and costume, thereby enacting a grotesque rehearsal of Vaughan's ultimate sex-death.

Throughout the whole novel, the car crash metaphor is used as a means of investigating the latent and manifest meanings of our technological culture, as well as the relationship between violence and sexual fantasies. For Vaughan, the wounds resulting from automobile disasters are 'the keys to a new sexuality born from a perverse technology' (C. 13). Through him, Ballard claims to have discovered 'the meaning of whiplash injuries and roll-over, the ecstasies of head-on collisions' (C. 10). As was the case in *The Atrocity Exhibition*, violence and perversion seem to have become the only means through which Ballard's characters can relate to each other or even achieve a sense of transcendence, if only by 'breaking through the skin of reality and convention' (R/S 47). Vaughan's obsessive longing for the eroticized atrocities of car crash injuries invites comparison with the Marquis de Sade, whose interest in discovering the seeds of the psychopathologies of his age and cataloguing all forms of erotic pleasure was equally unembarrassed by traditional moral considerations. To Ballard, Vaughan and the other characters in the novel, the car crash appears primarily as a means of triggering new sensations which would enable them to escape the burden of their psychic past and enliven a sexual life that has become sterile and perfunctory.

The narrator's perception, near the end of the novel, of 'the skid lines and loops of bloodstained oil' near an accident site as 'the choreographic codes of a complex gun battle, the diagram of an assassination attempt' is symptomatic of his desire to turn the car crash into a means of re-enacting a rite of passage through which to rehearse the premises of 'a new currency of pain and desire' (C. 153, 134). Ballard's fascination with the stylized violence of the car crash leads him to visualize a seemingly endless catalogue of violent deaths, each of which contains the terms of its own secret logic. These speculations give rise to a series of repertories of accident positions and bodily deformities based on a number of real and imagined scenarios, the sum of which somehow results in a union of blood, semen and gasoline that proclaims 'the marriage of sex and technology'. One of the most intriguing features of the novel results from the narrator's interest in the aftermath of the car crash and his detailed description of the characters' scars and injuries. Like so many other things in Crash, the painstaking precision of Ballard's descriptions of crash-inflicted wounds and dislocated bodies (which is largely inspired by photographs contained in Jacob Kulowski's medical text book Crash Injuries) proves both fascinating and repellent. But perhaps the most unexpected turn taken by the narrative lies in Ballard's translation of the crash-inflicted wounds into symbols of an oncoming process of bodily and spiritual transfiguration. Indeed, Ballard sees the scars and injuries on his own body, as well as on the bodies of all present and future crash victims, as the promise of 'a new generation of wounds' that might create 'contact points for all the sexual possibilities of their futures' and, ultimately, 'solve the codes of a deviant technology' (C. 135, 156, 194).

According to the Preface to the first French edition of the novel, the pornography and violence of *Crash* was intended to be used for 'cautionary' purposes. The novel as a whole, Ballard insists, is 'a warning against that brutal, erotic and overlit realm that beckons more and more persuasively to us from the margins of the technological landscape' (R/S 98). As suggested above, however, the moral element seems absent from the novel to the extent that it never passes judgement on the characters' behaviours – their capacity to follow their obsessions to their logical end therefore establishes itself as the norm by which to appraise their own lives and the reality of the novel as a whole. If Ballard's book has a political or 'cautionary' purpose, it is not so much to be found in the author's alleged indictment of the perversion of modern technology as in the latter's collusion with the forces of death and negation that drive contemporary society.[1] A major underlying thesis of the novel is that the metastatic multiplication of images in our mass media world and the subsequent trivialization of war, murder and rape have given rise to a new semi-unconscious logic of violence, whose affectless condition Ballard had already started to explore in *The Atrocity Exhibition*. Reflecting on his wife's growing tenderness towards him and his body, Ballard sees himself as 'a kind of emotional cassette, taking [his] place with all those scenes of pain and violence that illuminated the margins of our lives – television newsreels of wars and student riots, natural disasters and police brutality.... This violence experienced at so many removes had become intimately associated with [their] sex acts' (C. 37). If Ballard's experience of violence and brutality had so far been safely confined to the depthless images of his TV screen, his own pain as he lies in the hospital bed now seems an extension of 'that real world of violence calmed and tamed within our television programmes and the pages of the news magazines' (C. 37). Lastly, Ballard's professional occupation as a producer of high-budget television commercials reasserts the centrality of the mass-media landscape to Ballard's vision of the late-twentieth-century self.

Ballard's vision of human relationships as directed by the

intersecting vectors of sex, speed, violence and technology has earned him a reputation as a precursor of cyberpunk literature. In more general terms, Ballard's novel offers a vision of the contemporary self that tends to embrace change rather than resist it. In the same way as the patients in *The Atrocity Exhibition* seem to surrender to the arid psychological landscapes of the postindustrial condition, the individual's capacity, in *Crash*, to adjust to the technological and environmental metamorphoses undergone by our society is presented as an integral part of a new set of social relationships. The result, for many of Ballard's characters, is a profoundly untragic nemesis – an emotional void in which any attempt to rebel against the current (dis)order of things is immediately nipped in the bud, often in a subliminal way, by the invisible persuasive powers of our everyday environment. Deprived of its physical and psychological integrity, the subject becomes a mere constellation of signs which the artist-as-semiotician is supposed to decode and interpret in terms of its relationship to the collective unconscious of the contemporary age.

At this stage, one must point out that *Crash* is deprived of the anti-technological bias of, say, a Ralph Nader, whose indictment of the deadly effects of technology in *Unsafe at Any Speed* was repeatedly denounced by Ballard as the work of a dangerous opportunist 'using the psychological weaponry of fear and anxiety' (*UGM* 259). For, despite its original purpose as a 'cautionary' novel, its interest in the effect of technology on human consciousness and its choice of the car as the supreme emblem of a mass-merchandized machine of violence, *Crash* refuses to participate in the anxious alarmism of anti-technological lobbies. On the contrary, it sets out to pursue the inventory of 'benevolent' and 'benign' technologies which, for Ballard, constitute the promise of 'a new marriage of sensation and possibility' (C. 80, 162, 106). Ballard's position in this matter can be usefully related to Marshall McLuhan's view of 'the fusion of sex and technology'[2] as originating in an insatiable desire to explore new sexual possibilities by technological means, on the one hand, and eroticize our relationship with machines, on the other.

At the end of the novel, Ballard becomes increasingly attracted to the prospect of his own death in a car collision. As he is

AN ALPHABET OF WOUNDS

'designing the elements of [his] own car-crash', the traffic keeps moving and the novel ends in a vision of the rescue aircraft 'carrying the remnants of Vaughan's semen to the instrument panels and radiator grilles of a thousand crashing cars, the leg stances of a million passengers' (C. 224). Finally, the mystical tones of the narrator's apocalyptic visions of the ultimate 'autogeddon' carry ambiguous connotations of transfiguration and recovery, as epitomized in the narrator's LSD-induced vision of 'the brightness of the traffic ... celebrating the unity of [his] crash and this metallized Elysium' (C. 106, 198). The transfiguring powers of the car crash were already apparent in Dr Nathan's comments, in *The Atrocity Exhibition*, that 'apart from its manifest function, redefining the elements of space and time in terms of our most potent consumer durable, the car crash may be perceived unconsciously as a fertilizing rather than a destructive event' (*AE* 19). If the original purpose of Ballard's novel was to expose the 'voyeurism, self-disgust, the infantile basis of our dreams and longings' (*R/S* 96), the car, in *Crash*, eventually becomes the symbol of a more positive mediation not only between the characters' minds and bodies but also between their basest instincts and their thirst for spiritual renewal. Apparently responding to a reality altered by self-destructive forces inherent in their own selves, they nevertheless welcome the prospect of a certain form of spiritual recovery and psychic fulfilment which is yet to be discovered in the 'racing alphabets' (C. 197) formed by the accelerating cars. Their entranced surrender to the implacable logic of the car crash becomes an initiation into a radically new environment, a process Ballard describes in terms that frequently combine the raw intensities of sexual energy and religious revelation:

> Around me the interior of the car glowed like a magician's bower, the light within the compartment becoming darker and brighter as I moved my eyes. The instrument dials irradiated my skin with their luminous needles and numerals. The carapace of the instrument binnacle, the inclined planes of the dashboard panel, the metal sills of the radio and ashtrays gleamed around me like altarpieces, their geometries reaching towards my body like the stylized embraces of some hyper-cerebral machine. (C. 200)

This excerpt clearly demonstrates that the narrator's fascination with violent death and self-inflicted mutilation should not be interpreted merely as a symptom of his sadomasochistic tendencies but, rather, as the manifestation of a spiritual transformation which has already taken place in the characters' minds. The ultimate purpose of Ballard's attempts to decipher the language of scars and wound-profiles is to grasp the true nature of a reality in which the automobile crash – along with other real or imagined scenarios of decay and technological destruction – can provide a focus for an analysis of a wide range of conflicting impulses involving the uneasy cohabitation of strange, unsettling acts of sexuality and physical violence, as well as the perspective of self-sacrifice and psychological deliverance. As suggested by the 'mirror of blood, semen and vomit' produced by Catherine Ballard following her husband's 'first minor collision' in a hotel car-park (the image echoes the 'mirror smeared with vomit' appearing to Travis in the opening section of *The Atrocity Exhibition*, p. 10), what is also at stake in Ballard's poetics of abjection is the creation of a new grammar of (self-)representation that does justice to the characters' altered values and perspectives. Ballard's description of this 'magic pool', in which he sees his own reflection, as 'lifting from her throat like a rare discharge of fluid from the mouth of a remote and mysterious shrine' (*C.* 16) once again emphasizes the deep religious intensity of his responses to the violent energies released by the car crash.

But the automobile is not just an extension of the characters' bodies and personalities, or an outlet for repressed sexual urges and latent religious feelings. Ballard's characters indeed crave for a complete identification with the cold, impersonal energy of machines, thereby following a process discussed above as reflecting a Freudian displacement of affect and its subsequent annihilation into the nonorganic. (Such a reifying impulse had, of course, been there all along in Ballard's fiction since the mineral landscapes of *The Drought* and *The Crystal World*.) The fusion of body and machine finds its most absolute expression in Ballard's account of an LSD trip that functions as a prelude to his 'solid', cyborgian fusion with the automobile. Towards the end of the novel, Ballard is guided by Vaughan along an expressway that becomes a symbolic landscape. Whereas the changing perspective of the motorway transforms its concrete walls into 'luminous cliffs', the cars on the motorway (which Ballard describes elsewhere as 'the welcoming centaurs of some Arcadian land' and 'an armada of angelic creatures, each surrounded by an immense corona of light', C. 166, 199), appear 'delighted as dolphins' swimming through 'the golden air' (C. 196):

> Looking around, I had the impression that all the cars on the highway were stationary, the spinning earth racing beneath them to create an illusion of movement. The bones of my forearms formed a solid coupling with the shift of the steering column, and I felt the smallest tremors of the roadwheels magnified a hundred times, so that we traversed each grain of gravel or cement like the surface of a small asteroid. The murmur of the transmission system reverberated through my legs and spine, echoing off the plates of my skull as if I myself were lying in the transmission tunnel of the car, my hands taking the torque of the crankshaft, my legs spinning to propel the vehicle forwards. (C. 196–7)

Alternating between extremes of baseness and spirituality, collapsing traditional distinctions between the abject and the spiritual, the artificial and the natural, *Crash* is characterized by a desire to break through the limits of consciousness and an irresistible urge to accept the instrumental logic of the automobile as an opportunity to attain what Ballard terms 'the borderzones of identity' (C. 49). In the light of Ballard's suggestion that technology might contain the seeds of a new kind of mysticism,[3] the most significant literary ancestor of *Crash* is not de Sade but Henry Adams who, as early as 1900, saw in the 'ultimate energy'[4] and 'occult mechanism'[5] of the dynamo a privileged locus for the interpenetration of physical, sexual and religious energies. One is also reminded of Filippo Tommaso Marinetti's *Futurist Manifesto* (1909) and its celebration of the 'famished roar of the automobiles'[6] as the key to the emergence of a new-born self nourished by the beauty of technology and speed. If one considers the specific cultural and historical context out of which *Crash* emerged, however, Ballard's affinities are once again with the art world rather than the literary scene. Despite his indebtedness to Burroughs and Genet, his sensibility may be closer to that of sculptors such as Eduardo Paolozzi (himself a regular contributor to Moorcock's *New Worlds*) and John Chamberlain (whose sculptures made from parts of wrecked automobiles started to appear in the early

1960s), with whom he shares a fascination with the machine-influenced logic of consumer culture. Besides Ballard's own crashed car exhibition held at the London News Arts Laboratory in 1969 (which will be discussed in a later chapter), another interesting precedent was Jim Dine's happening *The Car Crash* (1960), which was intended to create a ritualized performance of the sensations produced by a traffic incident. Ballard's interest in the visual arts also led to a series of 'collages' published in the late 1960s and early 1970s in Martin Bax's magazine *Ambit*, to which Paolozzi was then a contributing editor. Ballard's collages – which consist of photograph enlargements and slogans in block-letters – were meant as a series of 'mock-advertisements' for which he paid the regular commercial rate. They were part of an ironic attempt to put conventional marketing strategies to the service of the basic concepts expressed in his fiction. One of the manifesto-like commercials Ballard published in *Ambit*, entitled 'The Angle Between Two Walls', reads like a summary of the central ideas underlying Ballard's *Crash*: 'Fiction is a branch of neurology: the scenarios of nerve and blood vessel are the written mythologies of memory and desire' (*R/S* 149).

In *Concrete Island* (1974), Ballard's second 'crash novel', the architect Robert Maitland has a tire blow-out while driving at full speed, and crashes his car onto a patch of wasteland. The entire action of the novel takes place on this 'small traffic island, some two hundred yards long and triangular in shape, that lay in the waste ground between three converging motorway routes' (*CI* 10). An injury to his leg and the indifference of the passing drivers prevent Maitland from escaping, and he progressively comes to accept the situation as he remains marooned on the island for the duration of the novel. The synopsis of *Concrete Island* immediately evokes the myth of Robinson Crusoe. Maitland, however, is closer to the hero of Michel Tournier's adaptation of the Crusoe story in *Vendredi ou les limbes du Pacifique* than to Defoe's protagonist. An inverted Robinson, Maitland does not try to recreate a civilized society on a miniature scale but, instead, goes through a process of initiation that draws him away from civilization into the deepest and most primitive reaches of his unconscious self. In a typically Ballardian manner, Maitland's journey 'Through the Crash

Barrier' (*CI* 7) signals the emergence of a new identity in himself, one which is more or less dictated to him by reminiscences of his childhood, on the one hand, and by a confrontation with the subconscious energies of his inner self, on the other. Like the protagonist of *Crash*, Maitland – who also leads a relatively ordinary suburban married life which he has come to perceive as increasingly unsatisfying – soon realizes that he himself has 'almost deliberately created this situation, as if preparing for his crash' (*CI* 21). (This ambiguous moment of insight is shared, to some extent, by many of Ballard's protagonists, who often tend to subconsciously trigger off their own private 'catastrophe'.)

Examining his reflection in the driving mirror after the crash, Maitland sees his eyes staring back at him, 'blank and unresponsive, as if he were looking at a psychotic twin brother' (*CI* 8). A few minutes later, he sees in the polished surface of the rear wheel-housing a distorted image of himself: 'His tall figure was warped like a grotesque scarecrow, and his white-skinned face bled away in the curving contours of the bodywork. A madman's grimace, one ear on a pedicle six inches from his head' (C. 12). Maitland's sense of duality and self-estrangement, apparent in the two opening 'mirror scenes' of the novel, is also reflected in his interaction with the two original 'rulers' of the island, Jane Sheppard and Proctor, both of whom are mentally unbalanced and bring out 'unwelcome strains' (*CI* 126) in his character. By so doing, they also evoke the unconscious drives (often symbolized by the dense vegetation covering the concrete island) Maitland has so far tried to repress. Proctor himself is a dual figure who appears now as an 'aged defective, knocked about by a race of unkind and indifferent adults but still clinging to his innocent faith in a simple world', now as a 'punch-drunk sparring partner who has gone the hard way' (*CI* 62, 63). His antagonistic position towards Ballard's protagonist is expressed in his acrobatic turns which Maitland sees as a ritualized attempt to channel 'a long-borne hostility to the intelligent world on which he would happily revenge himself' (*CI* 69). As for Jane Sheppard, she is alternately described as 'a caricature of a small-town forties whore' and an emotionally bruised woman-child whose face bears an expression of 'naïve corruption' (*CI* 64, 73). Her initial warmth and

43

attention soon turn into anger and resentment against Maitland, whom she comes to identify with the father of her dead child.[7]

As the island becomes 'an exact model of his head' (*CI* 51), Maitland's expedition becomes a journey through his own past. Thinking about his relationship to his wife and son, he sees his adulthood as a protracted attempt to 'remythologize his own childhood':

> The image in his mind of a small boy playing endlessly by himself in a long suburban garden surrounded by a high fence seemed strangely comforting. It was not entirely vanity that the framed photograph of a seven-year-old boy in a drawer of his desk at the office was not of his son, but of himself. Perhaps even his marriage to Catherine, a failure by anyone else's standards, had succeeded precisely because it recreated for him this imaginary empty garden. (*CI* 22)

Maitland progressively comes to identify the island itself with his lost childhood Golden Age and, later, with his own newly transfigured self ('I am the island', *CI* 52). From then on, his desire to escape becomes a less important goal than the need to survive and take possession of the island. After a number of unsuccessful attempts to call for help, Maitland goes as far as dismissing the assumption that sooner or later he will be rescued by a passing driver as 'part of that whole system of comfortable expectations he had carried with him' (*CI* 32) Likewise, he begins to forget his wife and son, as well as his lover Helen Fairfax and his partners, who have moved back 'into the dimmer light at the rear of his mind, their places taken by the urgencies of food, shelter, his injured leg and, above all, the need to dominate the patch of ground immediately around him' (*CI* 66–7). After having inspected the territory carefully, he realizes that the island itself has a history that dates from before World War II, and identifies the remains of a churchyard, a number of Edwardian terraced houses, air-raid shelters and the ruins of a local cinema which Jane and Proctor have turned into a permanent shelter. In the meantime, Maitland is discovering that the island is larger than he had first thought: 'The island seemed larger and more contoured, a labyrinth of dips and hollows. The vegetation was wild and lush, as if the island was moving back in time to an earlier and more violent period' (*CI* 74).

Maitland eventually welcomes this opportunity to discover his true self. His unexpected surge of moral courage also coincides with his deliverance from the fetters of measured time. In a symbolic gesture, Proctor rotates the hands of his watch at random, thereby confirming his essential role in introducing Maitland to a 'new time setting' (CI 86). More generally, the island awakens in him unknown energies that had until then lain buried under the weight of civilized rationality and affections, leaving him free 'to rove for ever within the empty city of his own mind' (CI 101). Maitland, who has now learnt to adapt himself and respond intuitively to his new surroundings (he also acquires Proctor's ability to read the grass by touch), seems to have inherited the island from its former masters. Having mastered his self-pity and seen in 'the resilience of [the island's] coarse grass...a model of behaviour and survival', Maitland manages to assert his ascendancy over Jane and Proctor by exploiting a strain of ruthlessness and cruelty that seems to develop from his new sense of empathy with the secret nature of the island, which he now perceives as an 'immense green creature eager to protect and guide him' (CI 43, 50). Significantly enough, Maitland's power to change 'the whole economy of [Proctor's] life' (CI 106) and turn him into a grotesque caricature of a civilized man (the tramp now takes wine with his meals and is wearing Maitland's dinner suit) directly depends on his capacity to exploit and humiliate him. Maitland's decision to teach Proctor how to write, however, signals the ultimate failure of civilization to provide any kind of help or relief on the island. In the chapter entitled 'The naming of the island', Ballard describes the tramp's brief apprenticeship in unusually moving terms. His eyes 'watering with pride' (CI 109), Proctor first seems exhilarated by the pleasure he finds in scrawling letters across the concrete. He then becomes determined to cover the whole of the island's surface with an indecipherable chain of letters which he assumes to be his name but which in fact consists of fragments of Maitland's own name. Proctor soon grows discouraged and it turns out that Maitland's attempts to civilize him are indirectly responsible for the tramp's death in a desperate attempt to leave the island.

After completing Proctor's burial, Maitland begins to gather new physical strength. He realizes that he can walk without the help of a crutch and tears away the remains of his ragged shirt in a final, affirmative gesture of self-liberation. He deliberately misses several opportunities to reach out for help and finally decides that 'in some ways the task he had set himself was meaningless', that he felt no real need to leave the island and that 'this alone confirmed that he had established his dominion over it' (*CI* 126). Curiously enough – at least by the standards set by the rest of the novel – the story nevertheless ends with Maitland's recognition that he will soon have to 'plan his escape from the island' and go back to his wife and son. Ballard does not give the reader any clue as to whether Maitland's sudden change of mind is to be taken in a positive or a negative sense within the context of his ongoing spiritual transfiguration. Since the novel leaves us with the impression that the process of psychic individuation triggered by the island has been successfully completed, Maitland's final decision to return to the civilized world may imply that his need to escape from the pressures of society and family was only a necessary stage he had to go through in order to give his life a new sense of direction and purpose.

Like many other works produced during what Martin Amis called Ballard's 'hard-edge, concrete-and-steel period',[8] Ballard's 'crash novels' are emblematic of Ballard's penchant for 'literary collages' made of images and ideas, rather than plots and fully-fledged characters; a tendency his fiction was to retain until *Empire of the Sun* and his more recent 'novels of ideas', *Rushing to Paradise* and *Cocaine Nights*. *Crash* and *Concrete Island* are also typical of how Ballard's novels and stories tend to focus on the isolated consciousness of a single (male) protagonist surrounded by a limited number of secondary characters whose double function is to stand for different facets of his divided psyche and prompt his oncoming spiritual metamorphosis. Ballard's central characters are almost invariably white, Anglo-Saxon, middle-class individuals. Their humdrum lives are suddenly interrupted by a crisis they seem to have longed for or provoked – if only unconsciously – and in the context of which they prove exceptionally lucid and resourceful. In most of the works examined so far, Ballard's protagonists all speak in a voice whose intensely self-reflexive and analytical tone is immediately recognizable. More often than not, they have a talent for introspective observation and tend to study their own obsessions and perversions with great, quasi-scientific exactness – hence, perhaps, the numerous doctors, scientists and architects who people Ballard's stories. As for Ballard's female characters, they often stand as rather effaced and elusive but nevertheless symbolically charged figures whose main function in the narrative is to elicit a particular emotional or intellectual response in the mind of the protagonist – one major exception to this rule being, of course, the figure of Dr Barbara in *Rushing to Paradise*. As David Pringle has observed, the commonest type of woman character in Ballard's fiction is derived from the distant, desirable and potentially threatening Jungian Anima figure. Like Jane Sheppard in *Concrete Island*, Ballard's female characters represent different aspects of the 'dark lamia' embodied by Gabrielle Szabo in 'The Day of Forever'.[9] Other character types functioning as 'projections of desires and fears'[10] of the protagonist include a number of lower-class characters who, like Proctor, are usually portrayed as hostile, menacing and uncommunicative creatures.

Ballard's failure to create credible and sophisticated female or non-middle-class characters, as well as his tendency to reduce human beings to disembodied symbols and cling to a number of characterological and narrative stereotypes, will appear to some as a serious flaw in his novels. Others will argue that these limitations are compensated for by the visual richness and symbolic consistency of his work. Indeed, one of the most haunting and powerful aspects of Ballard's fiction derives precisely from the author's willingness to rely on his current obsessions and follow them to their logical end. The same applies to Ballard's tendency to stick to the same archetypal pattern and work it out again and again in a multitude of ways that, as we will see, prove mutually productive to a reader familiar with the different 'phases' of his oeuvre. In this respect, also, Ballard's frequent references to such primal narratives as the Bible or Shakespeare's *Tempest* clearly indicate that his purpose is not to perpetuate stereotypes but to make archetypal figures of the past relevant to our present condition.

5

Suburban Nightmares

In *High-Rise* (1975), Ballard continues his descriptive investigations of the latent effects of modern technology on the human mind and civilization's attempts to suppress the energies of the unconscious. The disaster synopsis of the novel involves this time the inhabitants of the 'vertical city' (*HR* 9), a forty-storey high-rise block, who gradually lose contact with the civilized world and revert to the latent primitive violence of the urban jungle. The opening paragraph of the novel indicates a return to the caustic, Beckettian humour and absurdist logic to be found in some of Ballard's early short stories, such as 'Mr. F. is Mr. F.' and 'Time of Passage':

> Later, as he sat on his balcony eating the dog, Dr Robert Laing reflected on the unusual events that had taken place within this huge apartment building during the previous three months. Now that everything had returned to normal, he was surprised that there had been no obvious beginning, no point beyond which their lives had moved into a clearly more sinister dimension. (*HR* 7)

High-Rise also differs from Ballard's previous concrete-and-steel stories in its use of a third-person narrative exploring a growing sense of isolation and alienation in the minds of three different characters. The first one, Dr Robert Laing, is a recently divorced senior lecturer at a nearby medical school who has sold his former house and moved to an apartment located on the twenty-fifth floor of the high-rise complex, which he has chosen 'specifically for its peace, quiet and anonymity' (*HR* 7). The second major character, a restless and promiscuous television producer named (rather appropriately) Richard Wilder, lives with his wife and two sons on the second floor of the building. At the beginning of the story, Wilder is working on a television documentary about the psychological risks of living in high-rise condominiums. The third figure of importance is the architect Anthony Royal, who was a member of the consortium which designed the high-rise. Royal, who is recovering from a recent car crash, occupies a penthouse apartment in the building. One of the main advantages of Ballard's choice of three main characters in *High-Rise* is that it affords us three different 'professional' points of view: Laing, Wilder and Royal respond to the catastrophe in a way that emphasizes their allegiance to systems of thought imposed upon them by the language of science, of the media and of modern architecture, respectively. As we will see, the high-rise divides itself into three social groups (also represented by Laing, Wilder and Royal), thus negating its original ethos as a perfect model of social homogeneity. As Laing comments, however, the main attraction of the high-rise initially lies in the fact that it affords its occupants 'the pleasures of a subtle kind of anonymity' (*HR* 9):

> By the usual financial and educational yardsticks [the two thousand tenants of the apartment building] were probably closer to each other than the members of any conceivable social mix, with the same tastes and attitudes, fads and styles – clearly reflected in the choice of automobiles in the parking-lots that surrounded the high-rise, in the elegant but somehow standardized ways in which they furnished their apartments, in the selection of sophisticated foods in the supermarket delicatessen, in the tones of their self-confident voices.

Attempting to rationalize his decision to leave his Chelsea house and move to the high-tech and high-security environment of the apartment building, Laing concludes that the high-rise is 'a huge machine designed to serve, not the collective body of tenants, but the individual resident in isolation' (*HR* 10). Indeed, perhaps the most important feature of the building – besides its relative social and architectural uniformity – is that it constitutes a completely self-sufficient whole comprising one thousand apartments and equipped with every modern convenience, a restaurant, a supermarket, a gymnasium, a small movie theatre, several swimming pools, a junior school and even a private bank. It soon becomes clear to Laing and the other characters that the apparent equilibrium of the apartment building is constantly on the verge of being destroyed by a growing number of minor confrontations, frustrations and personal rivalries lurking beneath an illusion of civility and normalcy.

The first significantly ominous incident which signals the approaching violence is the discovery of a dead Afghan hound in the centre of one of the swimming pools. Following the drowning of the dog (which, Laing immediately suspects, was a deliberate and provocative act), 'an almost palpable miasma' begins to cover the pool, 'as if the spirit of the drowned beast was gathering to itself all the forces of revenge and retribution present within the building' (HR 22). The drowning of the dog is only the first in a long series of violent reactions to the new atmosphere of distrust and hostility, including various acts of sabotage, vandalism, physical aggression, and sexual misdemeanour. As a result of this sudden surge of atavistic violence, the high-rise becomes the site of a conflict between the coercive structure of the building and the pressure of individuality and narcissism. The situation becomes so intolerable that even Royal himself, who starts to realize that his creation is assuming the form of a 'fur-lined prison', feels 'crushed by the pressure of all the people above him, by the thousands of individual lives, each with its pent-up time and space' (HR 81, 88). Typically, the crisis which affects the closed society of the high-rise is seen to arise from the hidden motives of its creator, and Royal is eventually forced to conclude that 'without knowing it, he had constructed a giant vertical zoo, its hundreds of cages stacked above each other' (HR 134).

Throughout the novel, the high-rise is used by Ballard as a social laboratory of the (near) future in which all the pretensions to stability and rationality of modern democracy are tested against a number of obsessions and speculations that have preoccupied him since the late 1950s. Implicit in Ballard's dystopian fable is the way in which the new man-made environment panders to a number of archetypal anxieties and perversities, some of which may lead to the final disintegration of the 'social contract' that binds the characters to each other. One of the underlying 'theses' of the novel is indeed that the structures and mechanisms which regulate our late-twentieth-century societies deny our deepest unconscious needs in the name of security and order. *High-Rise* therefore suggests that such societies are never immune to a return of the repressed, the scale of which will be directly proportional to the degree of physical and spiritual confinement of the individual.

In this respect, Ballard's investigation of the mind-deadening effects of suburban domestic life – a theme he was to further develop in *The Unlimited Dream Company* – is linked with an understanding of the fundamental failure of technology to provide any more than a precarious social and psychological status quo; one whose instrumental rationality is eventually eradicated by the violence it has sought to repress. Like the patients at 'The Intensive Care Unit', another short story concerned with the effects of technology as an instrument of psychic oppression (see below), the tenants of Ballard's *High-Rise* live in a seemingly timeless vacuum overrun by the reassuring, rectilinear functionalism and determinism of their high-tech, convenience-obsessed environment. Their sense of intellectual and emotional isolation – as well as the ensuing eruption of long-pent-up savagery that ensues – indeed results primarily from the 'never-failing supply of care and attention' (*HR* 10) provided by the new technological landscape and its endless possibilities for immediate gratification. The next step in this dehumanizing process is the ultimate psychological death of a self engulfed in a realm of absolute mental and physical autarchy that soon proves unviable. Because of their lack of social awareness and their absolute dependence on the services provided by the condominium, the tenants of the high-rise block, who behave 'like an advanced species of machine in the neutral atmosphere' (*HR* 35), also '[thrive] on the rapid turnover of acquaintances, the lack of involvement with others, and the total self-sufficiency of lives which, needing nothing, were never disappointed'. Having reached this post-Darwinian stalemate, the high-rise paradoxically relieves its occupants from 'the need to repress every kind of anti-social behaviour', leaving them 'free to explore any deviant or wayward impulses' (*HR* 36). What follows is a fascinating account of their attempts to adjust to the new laws dictated by the civil strife within the high-rise by indulging in a variety of sadistic rituals and transgressive sex acts that seem to sustain their will to survive. The story ends with Wilder's death at the hands of a group of cannibalistic women, which is followed by Laing's search for a new equilibrium based on an alternative, post-Freudian form of matriarchy in which he plays the roles of both lover and child.

The issue of class division (which, as we have seen, is conspicuously absent from Ballard's earlier novels) surfaces in the multi-layered world of the high-rise block. The occupants of the apartment building are well-to-do urban professionals living on different floors corresponding to their social and economic status. Far from being levelled out by the collective psychosis to which all of the tenants fall victim, these differences are further reinforced by the emergence of a social order organized around tribal allegiances and a number of competing private militia. As Laing's ideal of the absolute social uniformity of the high-rise begins to disintegrate, new power hierarchies based on capital and self-interest reassert themselves. Whereas the lower nine floors, Wilder observes, are inhabited by a '"proletariat" of film-technicians, air-hostesses and the like' whose 'territorial instinct...ha[s] atrophied to the point where they [are] ripe for exploitation', the middle section of the high-rise, which extends from the tenth floor to the swimming pool and restaurant deck on the 35th, is formed by a 'middle class, made up of self-centered but basically docile members of the professions – doctors and lawyers, accountants and tax specialists who worked, not for themselves, but for medical institutes and large corporations' (HR 54, 53). Above them, the top five floors are occupied by a 'discreet oligarchy of minor tycoons and entrepreneurs, television actresses and careerist academics' whose domination over the inferior levels is maintained with the help of a 'constantly dangling carrot of friendship and approval' (HR 53).

With this rather pessimistic vision of social relationships, *High-Rise* temporarily brings to a close Ballard's investigation of the marriage of technology, sex and violence begun with *The Atrocity Exhibition*. As we have seen, what remains confined to the level of the isolated consciousness in Ballard's previous novels here becomes part of a larger, social whole, a closed system whose 'eventless' (HR 52) dynamics result in the mutiny of a self which becomes oblivious to its former identity and sets out to explore the darkest corners of the soul. A later novella, *Running Wild* (1989), is also about the release of unconscious desires in an (over-)civilized environment. It investigates the massacre of all the adult residents of an elegant and placid suburban housing community, murdered at the hands of their own children. The children's rebellion against 'the regime of kindness and care' (*RW* 72) installed at Pangbourne Village by their enlightened and loving parents (all of whom share 'liberal and humane values displayed almost to a fault', *RW* 10) can only be accounted for in the context of a community which, like that of Ballard's *High-Rise*, is remarkable for having reached a state of optimal security, efficiency and self-sufficiency. Characteristically, the children's decision to escape from 'a non-stop diet of love and understanding' into 'a more brutal and more real world of the senses' (*RW* 46) originates in their parents' over-zealous efforts to ensure their education and well-being. The discovery of a mutilated Piaget book in a bedroom occupied by one of the children suggests that the Pangbourne massacre might stand for a rebuttal of all progress-oriented philosophies emphasizing the progressive socialization of the self and the ability of children to assimilate and perfect pre-existing schemes through their interaction with adult members of the community. Contrary to Jean Piaget's view of intellectual growth as a continuous progression towards rationality, Ballard's approach remains, as always, Freudian-based, in that it privileges a conception of psychic and social development which is constantly challenged by the pressures of regression and devolution.

6

Through the Crash Barrier

Many of the novels and short stories discussed so far indicate that Ballard's fiction, despite its dystopian premises, is often concerned with the possibility of attaining a superior state of awareness by breaking through the boundaries that separate the conscious from the unconscious mind. One of the clearest and fullest expressions of the continuing struggle taking place within the human psyche between the conscious, rational presence of the ego and the secret forces of the buried self is enacted in 'The Terminal Beach', a short story originally published in *New Worlds* in 1964. The protagonist, a former military pilot named Traven, has been driven by some private unconscious drive to the island of Eniwetok. There, he embarks on a quest for his dead wife and 6-year-old son, who were killed in a car accident. A biologist and his assistant, an unnamed young woman, meet him and help him by attending to his injured foot. In a manner reminiscent of Maitland's patient and obsessive resignation in *Concrete Island*, Traven eludes a search party that has come to find him and, sustained by memories and visions of his wife and son, decides to stay among the abandoned towers, blockhouses and bunkers located at the centre of the island, which also bears the scars of the atomic and hydrogen weapons tests carried out by the American government in the years that followed World War II. Responding to the complex and ambiguous sensations triggered by the island, Traven proceeds with his quest for a state of absolute forgiveness and self-forgetfulness, his awareness reduced to 'the few square inches of sand beneath his feet' (*BSS* 255). He later discovers the corpse of a Japanese man named Dr Yasuda, with whom he attempts to communicate. In what appears to be a parody of a Taoist parable, the dead man replies and recommends to Traven 'a philosophy of acceptance' that would enable him to recognize in the desolate landscape of Eniwetok 'an ontological Garden of Eden' (*BSS* 263).

The role of the inner world of the psyche as a communicating link with a prelapsarian reality and a source of spiritual power is also at the heart of *The Unlimited Dream Company* (1979), which signals an important turning point in Ballard's career. In this work, some of the major themes of his earlier novels – including the motifs of personal transformation, expanded consciousness, violence, sexuality and the characteristic opening 'crash' scene – start to be subjected to a much more positive and, some will argue, more optimistic treatment. Blake, the protagonist and narrator of the novel, is a young man who decides to steal a light plane from Heathrow Airport and crashes it into the Thames in the London suburb of Shepperton, Ballard's place of residence since the mid-1950s and the geographical and conceptual epicentre of many of his works. Blake miraculously survives his physical death in the accident and turns into a messianic figure endowed with supernatural powers. Within a few days, Blake, who discovers that his mind is capable of turning his dreams into reality, transforms the dull and conservative town of Shepperton ('the everywhere of suburbia, the paradigm of nowhere', *UDC* 35) into an immense Edenic tropical garden. (Throughout the novel, it remains unclear whether Blake's miracles actually occur in reality or in a peculiar kind of extended post-mortem dream fantasy.) Blake's dreams acquire a collective significance as the whole Shepperton population gradually revert to prelapsarian times and wander around naked and unaware of their nakedness, responding both to an irresistible spiritual desire for transcendence and to the advent of a strong and open sexuality.

The Unlimited Dream Company further establishes Ballard's predilection for the verticality of vision and allegory over the horizontal linearity of plot, as the major part of the novel is devoted to descriptions of Blake's mystico-sexual urges to transfigure the whole town of Shepperton and '[seed] in the wombs of its unsuspecting housewives a retinue of extravagant beings, winged infants and chimerized sons and daughters, plumed with the red and yellow feathers of macaws' (*UDC* 83). Blake – who, like Christ, performs miracles, including miraculous cures, and is eventually rejected and abused by those whom he has come to save – embodies extreme and mysteriously interactive forms of spiritualism and pansexuality. He is eventually killed by Stark (one of Ballard's typical 'flat', allegorical characters), a materialistic and greedy film stunt pilot who feels threatened by the new prevailing atmosphere of erotico-spiritual liberation. The inhabitants of Shepperton then resume their normal lives, despising and abusing their former idol. After his second death and resurrection through a series of alchemical transformations, Blake gathers new force from the animals and vegetation around him and manages to revive the whole town, sacrificing his last strengths to resuscitate Miriam St Cloud, a young woman doctor who appears as another incarnation of the Jungian lamia, an attractive though strangely antagonistic figure whom Blake sees alternately as a menacing witch and an emblem of benevolence and innocence. The following excerpt is one of several extended lyrical passages depicting Blake's capacity to assimilate the strength passed to him by the natural world:

> The forest was motionless. Every activity had ceased, the leaves and grass suspended in silence. I could feel the life flowing into me from all sides, willed to me by the smallest creatures and the lowliest. Together these simple beings were remaking me. The sparrows and thrushes passed their miniature retinas into my eyes, the voles and badgers within their burrows gave me their teeth, the elms and chestnuts willed their sap to me, grave wet-nurses running their milk into my body. Even the leeches on the propeller of the aircraft, the worms under my feet, the myriad bacteria in the soil were moving in a huge congregation through my flesh. A vast concourse of living beings crowded my arteries and veins, transforming the mortuary of my body with their life and goodwill. The cool moisture of snails irrigated my joints, I felt my muscles eased by the flexing of a thousand branches, my flesh balmed in the warm capillaries of a million sun-filled leaves ... I was born again from the lowest of the creatures, from the amoeba dividing in the meadow ponds, from the hydra and spirogyra. I was spawned by amphibians in the creek beside the meadow, and in the river as a dogfish from the body of my mother-shark. I was dropped by the pregnant deer on to the deep grass of the meadow. I emerged from the warm cloaca of birds. I was born by a thousand births from the flesh of every living thing in the forest, the father of myself. I became my own child. (*UDC* 199)

The figures of the 'grave wet-nurse' and the 'mother-shark' –

which relate to Blake's fear of being smothered by the affection of the Sheppertonians, like 'a deformed baby deliberately suffocated by loving relatives' (*UDC* 206) – point to the importance of the complex Freudian family romance that underlies Ballard's narrative. As is often the case in Ballard's fiction, it is only through the redistribution and permutation of traditional family roles within the same individual that the modern self can hope to achieve freedom from the life-denying pressures of society. Whereas the characters of Ballard's earlier novels tend to combine the roles of father/mother and child in order to ward off their private fears and adapt to the new parameters that rule their consciousness, the ultimate fusion of identities resulting from Blake's communion with the raw energy of nature ends all conflicting relationships between the adult individual and his former childhood self.

By the end of the novel, Blake has also become both a redeeming and a vampiric figure. He then realizes that his newly acquired pansexuality, and the various forms of perversion which accompany it (which include dreams of murder and paedophiliac urges) were only a prelude to his 'wedding' with the whole town, in which he sets out to absorb everyone in Shepperton and definitively escape from his former, corporeal self by achieving a god-like immortality. The motif of transcendence and collective transformation – already adumbrated by the orgasmic 'autogeddon' of *Crash* – is, so to speak, literalized when he decides to teach the inhabitants of the town to fly away from Shepperton towards the sun, forsaking what they now perceive as the mediocrity of their former lives. In a characteristically Ballardian apotheosis, Blake, who has given away his last strengths, appears confident in his dream of ascent and foresees the future departure of all the inhabitants of the Thames valley and of the world beyond:

> This time we would merge with the trees and the flowers, with the dust and the stones, with the whole of the mineral world, happily dissolving ourselves in the sea of light that formed the universe, itself reborn from the souls of the living who have happily returned themselves to its heart. Already I saw us rising into the air, fathers, mothers and their children, our ascending flights swaying across the surface of the earth, benign tornadoes hanging from the canopy of the universe, celebrating the last marriage of the animate and the inanimate, of the living and the dead. (*UDC* 220)

By the power of its luxuriant imagery and its sustained lyrical intensity, *The Unlimited Dream Company* unquestionably emerges as one of Ballard's most untypical, but also most successful, novels to date. Ballard – who throughout the 1970s had seemed less interested in redemption and reconciliation than in alienation and disorder – here describes the advent of a new psychopathology in unusually poetic terms which emphasize the creative and redeeming powers of the unconscious self, rather than its destructive and entropy-driven side. Characteristically, the primary goal of Blake's allegorical journey into the depths of the unconscious is the liberation and transformation of the individual consciousness, as well as the attainment of an absolute fusion of self and world. One realizes, at this stage, that Ballard's protagonist was most probably named after William Blake, whose equally equivocal bent towards eroticized mysticism also sought to inscribe the precultural self into the logic of contraries. Like Blake, Ballard creates a hymn to the wayward imagination in which all dualities – including that of body and soul – are dissolved into a single, all-encompassing flow of creative energy uncontaminated by the sustained orthodoxies of culture and society.

The Dionysian release provided by Blake's oneiric powers is indicative of Ballard's sense that our deeper self necessarily exceeds the limits of our ordinary intellectual and moral understanding. The suburban setting of the novel suggests that the buried energies of the unconscious or pre-conscious mind, including its Thanatotic desires, are never far below the surface of our everyday lives and are liable to disrupt our most fundamental assumptions concerning the nature of the real and our relationship to it. By bringing together affirmations of the highest spiritual ideals and the release of long-repressed sexual drives and perverse impulses, Blake's unlimited dreams also urge the reader to question culturally inherited notions of transformation and redemption, sin and retribution. For what emerges from the novel as a whole is the disturbing idea that the acceptance and, to some extent, the cultivation of our deepest needs for deviance and self-annihilation are a necessary condition – at least within the bounds of the individual consciousness – for the recovery of a pre-cultural grace, one in which sexual energy becomes a primeval territory of formative movement at the junction of being and non-being.

7

The Loss of the Real

With *Hello America* (1981), Ballard takes his SF readers back to the slightly more familiar realm of 'straight' speculative fiction. The story takes place some time in the late twenty-first century and concerns a scientific expedition sent from Europe to the American continent, which was deserted by its inhabitants after the total collapse of its fossil-fuel-based economies a few decades earlier. Ballard proceeds to explore the nature of the American dream, namely 'the proposition that everyone should be able to live out his further fantasies, wherever they might lead, explore every opportunity, however bizarre' (*HA* 106). It becomes clear from the outset that the members of the expedition, who are all of American ancestry, have brought their personal baggage of hopes and ambitions to this country of intense possibility. The common denominator of their dreams and aspirations is a sense of absolute freedom and a conviction that they can make a new life and fulfil themselves by responding to the sheer energy of the empty land. Wayne Fleming, the protagonist, is an 18-year-old stowaway on the ship, whose father disappeared during an earlier expedition to the American continent. Although he was originally drawn to America because of his craving for romance and adventure, his ultimate ambition is to become President of the United States. Unlike Wayne, who is described as 'a young redeemer with his planetary dreams of moving the seas and the winds', Captain Steiner, a former Israeli naval officer, seems to think of America as a vast open area that constitutes 'the ultimate backdrop to his fantasies of being alone' (*HA* 84, 87). Whereas Dr Paul Ricci has left his native Italy for fear of being disgraced following a professional scandal over his university's Library Fund, Gregor Orlowski, the 'political leader' of the expedition, is a Soviet bureaucrat who was sent to America against his will but who nevertheless dreams of becoming a major colonial administrator of a revived New York City. Lastly, Professor Anne Summers, an attractive radiologist brought up in the American ghetto in Berlin, is driven by a need to escape from the enclosed and restricted life of her Spandau flat and 'extend herself' (*HA* 30) in a land she sees as a place of unlimited space and energy.

The conceptual crux of the story is the expedition's encounter with one of Ballard's most successful psychopathological cases: a madman-recluse who has named himself Charles Manson and embodies the potentially self-destructive power of the American dream. Manson rules a new empire centred around Las Vegas, a make-believe world in which he uses a sophisticated laser holograph projector to fill the sky with thousand-foot-high images of Mickey Mouse, Marilyn Monroe, Superman, Coca Cola bottles, the Starship Enterprise, John Wayne, Lee Harvey Oswald and, finally, the original Charles Manson. Manson's holographic empire (whose headquarters are located in a replica of the Pentagon War Room in the sports pavilion of a Caesar's Palace hotel) can be usefully related to Ballard's more general concern with the proliferation of mass-media icons and the politics of postmodern simulation. In an article first published in a 1966 issue of *New Worlds*, Ballard claims that 'the fictional elements in the world around us are multiplying to the point where it is almost impossible to distinguish between the "real" and the "false"'. 'The faces of public figures', he continues, 'are projected at us as if out of some endless global pantomime, and have the conviction of giant advertisement hoardings' (*UGM* 88). Such comments are a striking example of how Ballard's critique of contemporary Western societies prefigures Jean Baudrillard's famous theories on the culture of 'hyperreality' and the 'loss of the real'.[1] The characters of *Hello America* once again teeter on the verge of this timeless space in which a surplus of televised images has allegedly erased all former notions of truth – they are caught up in a play of 'simulacra', copies that no longer refer to an original, images that no longer have any direct relationship with an outside, external world. In this virtual space of near-absolute simulation, the only alternative left to them is to realize their own fantasies and create their own particular version of reality. The process of simulation which, in the depthless fantasies of *The Atrocity Exhibition*, remains confined to a succession of symptoms identified in a series of isolated fantasies, becomes here part of a larger narrative framework which eventually leads to the imprisonment of psychic energy, now deadlocked into Manson's iconographic bulimia, his obsessive craving for power and his paranoid fears. In Ballard's post-humanist and post-historical vacuum, the passive consumption of mass-produced, ideologically-charged icons of popular Americana stands for the unconditional and uncritical surrender of the self to the glamour of a society saturated with depthless images and illusory fictions.

The inescapable logic of the simulacrum is present in a number of short stories published in the 1970s and 1980s. 'The Greatest Television Show on Earth' deals with the discovery of a system of time travel that provides television companies with an inexhaustible supply of violent and sensationalist entertainment. Because some of the 'live' coverage of famous historical events prove less spectacular than was originally expected, some companies go as far as to revamp a number of famous battles, such as the defeat of Napoleon Bonaparte at Waterloo, in order to boost audience ratings. In 'The Object of the Attack', the dangers of media manipulation are embodied in the figure of Colonel Thomas Jefferson Stamford, a former American astronaut who becomes the self-appointed TV messiah of a new 'space-based religion' (*WF* 57) leading a televised crusade against atheistic Marxism and the rest of the non-Christian world. Colonel Stamford, who resembles a cross between Billy Graham and Rasputin, is an extremely skilful and dangerous demagogue putting all the available media technology, including huge illusionist light-shows featuring laser holograms, at the service of 'a potent mix of evangelical Christianity, astronautics and cybernetic movie making' (*WF* 61). In 'The Secret History of World War 3', a story contained in *War Fever* (1990), Ballard's most recent collection to date, a suburban paediatrician living near Washington DC reports on a brief nuclear confrontation between the United States and the former USSR during Ronald Reagan's third term of office. Because the nation's TV screens and leading newspapers are dominated almost exclusively by reports on the ailing president's health, World War III passes unnoticed by the great majority of American citizens. The continuous flow of information provided by the media on Reagan's physical and mental condition is in fact meant to distract the public's attention from a number of critical events taking place in the real world, including a falling stock market and the Soviet invasion of Pakistan which prompts the mobilization of NATO and Warsaw Pact reserve troops. Implicit in Ballard's story (which points forward, rather prophetically, to Jean Baudrillard's famous article 'The Gulf War Never Happened') is the suggestion that human consciousness is locked in a losing battle with invasive media technologies that are producing a generation of cultural dupes.

'Theatre of War' and 'War Fever' explore other types of worldwide conspiracy involving the manipulative strategies of government and the media. Whereas the first story is a futuristic account of civil strife in Britain cast in the form of an uninterrupted 'TV documentary, of the type made popular by *World in Action*' (*MNF* 118), the second is about an endless civil war taking place in Beirut, which turns out to be orchestrated by the United Nations as a gigantic experiment in the sociological and psychological origins of the 'virus of war' (*WF* 18). The continuation of the conflict is made possible only by means of a relentless propaganda campaign based on forged atrocity photographs and TV broadcasts playing on the citizens' personal fears, religious feelings and political ideals. 'The Life and Death of God' begins with the public announcement of the existence of an 'intelligent being of infinite dimensions' (*LFA* 139) residing in a complex electromagnetic system of microwaves pervading the entire universe. The discovery of this supreme 'sentient being' gradually invalidates all current religious and political systems, as a close examination of its 'presumed moral nature' leads scientists and religious leaders to the conclusion that its dimensions are 'large enough to embrace any interpretation one [cares] to invent' (*LFA* 138, 141). The absence of any moral directives from the Almighty causes the collapse of civilized life and eventually prompts theologians to publish a Christmas encyclical announcing God's death.

'Motel Architecture' and 'The 60 Minute Zoom' present extreme pathological examples of what media technology can do to the psyches and personalities of its users. 'Motel Architecture' relates the story of a man named Pangborn who spends most of his life in a solarium equipped with a dozen television screens displaying different sections of the shower sequence in Alfred Hitchcock's movie *Psycho*. After the years spent in the artificial world of the solarium, Pangborn becomes so detached from reality and estranged from himself that he eventually commits suicide to escape 'the intrusive fact of his own consciousness' (*MNF* 194). The narrator of 'The 60 Minute Zoom' is a man obsessed with the private behaviour of his neighbours and of his wife, upon whom he spies by means of a high-powered zoom camera. This growing obsession culminates in a desire to create 'the ultimate home movie', one in which 'the elements of [his wife's] infidelity become totally abstracted from themselves, areas of undifferentiated light that assuage all anger and regret' (*VH* 141). Like Pangborn in 'Motel Architecture', the narrator of Ballard's story is a self-divided being whose 'affectless' condition goes hand in hand with his incapacity to relate to himself and others except through the 'reductive authority' (*VH* 138) of the camera lens.

Other stories extend Ballard's concern with the new era of simulation, as well as with the effects of technological 'mediation' in the largest sense, to other fields of social life, such as the advances of medical science or space travel technology. In 'The Impossible Man', an early work contained in the collection *The Disaster Area*, the advances of modern surgery have made it possible to prolong life more or less indefinitely. As one of the characters of the story, Dr Matthews, remarks, an increasing number of patients refuse treatment because they find out that 'everything worthwhile has finite bounds' and that 'the hard lines drawn around things give them their identity' (*DA* 188). A more recent work, 'Memories of the Space Age', tells of the murder of an astronaut committed in front of millions of television witnesses. The murder (which is seen within the larger context of various psychological disturbances affecting the consciousnesses of all NASA employees) marks the end of the space age, which, in turn, comes to be seen as the product of a collective hubris and a logical consequence of an 'evolutionary crime' (*WF* 146) committed by the whole of mankind.

'Love in a Colder Climate' and 'The Intensive Care Unit' are superbly written psychological thrillers dealing with the mechanization of human relationships and our diminishing responses to 'real', unmediated life. The first story takes place in the twenty-first century, after the ravages of AIDS and a panoply of other mutating viruses have caused people to abstain from every kind of physical or sexual relationship. Faced with a plunging birth rate and the possibility of the extinction of mankind, the government decides that all fertile and healthy citizens will henceforth be required to take part in a programme of arranged sexual encounters. 'The Intensive Care Unit' envisions a society in which it is an indictable offence (mainly for reasons of security and hygiene) to meet another human being in person, so that human contacts are made possible only by means of television. An open-minded paediatrician who advocates closer intimacies in family life entertains the illicit notion of actually meeting his wife and children in the flesh. Unfortunately, the sudden eruption of conflicting feelings and Oedipal violence prompted by their encounter turns the long-awaited family reunion into a terrible slaughter. At a time when virtual sex has become the subject of endless speculation on the part of computer programmers and cultural theorists alike, Ballard's vision of the affectlessness and artificiality of human relationships takes on familiar connotations. More importantly, however, Ballard's dystopian propositions are typical of his desire to remap the changing trajectories of body and mind in a way that does justice to a whole range of new experiences left unexplored by most contemporary writers. The postulate that our sense of self is, to some extent, affected by such things as car crashes, high-rises, electronic media, supersonic jets, the prospect of a nuclear war and the large-scale entrance of mass-merchandized technology into our everyday lives, has indeed constituted the very methodological basis of Ballard's fiction since the late 1950s. The same principle applies, of course, to the relationship between fiction and the real – the latter being constantly reinvented and adapted to the new set of perspectives offered by what Ballard sees as a complex mesh of interconnecting environmental changes. As we have seen, Ballard constantly presents these changes as both the cause and the end-product of his characters' bizarre personalities –

according to which view, technology both meets and creates profound and irrepressible psychological needs at the same time as it affords us new strategies by which to cope with external social pressures.

In the light of his fascination with the popular iconography of postindustrial Western culture and the possible psychological and technological futures of mankind, one can easily understand why Ballard considers science fiction 'the true literature of the twentieth century... one of the few forms of modern fiction explicitly concerned with change – social, technological and environmental – and certainly the only fiction to invent society's myths, dreams and utopias' (*UGM* 14). If conventional, mass-market science fiction 'defines the popular imagination of the twentieth century', Ballard's own particular brand of speculative fiction does not limit itself to merely entertaining the minds of its readers. It also professes to set the terms for a literary medium that is less concerned with 'the nuances of human relationships' than with the possibility of 'plac[ing] a philosophical and metaphysical frame around the most important events within our lives and consciousness' – a feature Ballard sees as radically opposed to the 'retrospective bias' of the modernist novel and its obsession with introspection and 'the rationalization of guilt and estrangement' (*R/S* 96). By embracing the hallmarks of the postindustrial age (which include the energy of 'optimism, the iconography of mass merchandising, naivety and a guilt-free enjoyment of all the mind's possibilities'), such a literature is in a position to do justice to 'the dynamics of human societies... and man's place in the universe' (*R/S* 96–7).

Ballard's own efforts to turn the SF medium into a tool for sociological and metaphysical speculation reflects his growing impatience with what many have come to see as the self-crippling parochialism of English letters in the 1950s and 1960s – a tendency Ballard describes rather harshly as being dominated by 'an obsession with obscure social nuances, with the minutiae of everyday language and behaviour, and a moralizing concern for the limited world of their own parish that would do credit to an elderly spinster peering down at her suburban side-street' (*UGM* 137). Predictably, Ballard's own literary tastes indicate his penchant for a literature freed from the moral and psychological limitations of 'Little-Englandism'; one which derives its inspiration from outside the traditional ambit of English life. One of the most determining influences on Ballard's early writings was that of Graham Greene, whose work emerges as a significant exception to his general lack of interest in the postwar English novel. What Ballard admires in Greene's fiction is, above all, his capacity to refrain from moralizing about his characters, whose strengths and weaknesses are 'accepted without comment like the grease on the fan, the dirt under one's fingernails' (*UGM* 138–9). Ballard's interest in the process of mental or actual emigration by which his favourite novelists transcend the cultural premises of their native countries indirectly reminds us that he was born and raised in Shanghai and did not arrive in England before the age of 16. In order to come to a fuller understanding of Ballard's eccentric position within the history of contemporary British writing, we must now turn to the account he gave of his Shanghai childhood in *Empire of the Sun*.

8

From Shanghai to Shepperton

Empire of the Sun was based on Ballard's own childhood years in Japanese-occupied Shanghai. The author's fictionalized account of his youthful experiences in the Lunghua internment camp – where he was interned for nearly three years shortly after the attack on Pearl Harbor – is one of the most original avatars of the so-called 'death of affect', here exemplified by the boy's candidly amoral and semi-fantastic understanding of the war, including the daily routine of death and starvation at the Lunghua camp. Yet, despite Jim's overall insensibility to his own suffering and that of others, the result is somehow as emotionally unsettling as it is forcefully unsentimental. As the reader follows Jim's attempts to assign meaning to a meaningless environment and cope with each day of malnutrition and disease, *Empire of the Sun* also signals a further interiorization of some of Ballard's favourite themes. His treatment of the isolated, fragmented self, for example, is here directly inscribed in the very fabric of Jim's consciousness and, thereby, dispenses with the author's more habitual 'literalized' psychological landscapes. Similarly, the forceful honesty and the extraordinary sobriety of tone of Jim's narrative endows him with a psychological credibility quite unlike the abstract or allegorical phantoms which people some of Ballard's earlier works.

The impact of modern media on private and public consciousness, as well as the ideological misrepresentations according to which reality can be perceived, interpreted and fictionalized, are once again central to Ballard's novel, as, for instance, when Jim's mind attempts to 'separate the real war from the make-believe conflicts invented by Pathé and

Movietone' (*ES* 14). In contrast with the patriotic, glamorizing war of the newsreels, Jim observes that 'real war was the thousands of Chinese refugees dying of cholera in the sealed stockades at Pootung, and the bloody heads of communist soldiers mounted on pikes along the Bund. In a real war no one knew which side he was on, and there were no flags or commentators or winners. In a real war there were no enemies' (*ES* 14). In addition to its systematic dismantling of consoling and positive clichés about World War II, *Empire of the Sun* also contains many direct or indirect critical assessments of life in the International Settlement. In many ways, the cosy, insular microcosm the British business and administrative community in Shanghai had imposed upon itself until the outbreak of the war is as lethally limiting – at least from a spiritual point of view – as the sordid conditions in Lunghua camp. Later, the British prisoners' attempts to 'sustain the illusion that even in Lunghua camp the values of a vanished England still survived' (*ES* 190) appear to Jim as so many ways of shutting out the squalid conditions of the camp and remaining passive when they should be struggling to survive. Unlike the other British prisoners, whose minds and bodies have been lulled into apathy by 'the fifty-year-long party that had been Shanghai', Jim does his best to 'keep the camp going, whatever the cost' (*ES* 225). As he begins to experience the harsh conditions of life in occupied Shanghai, Jim also comes to the conclusion that the values of heroism, kindness and self-sacrifice which his parents and teachers had always sought to inculcate in him mean very little in an environment ruled by falsehood, cruelty and self-interest. The more positive aspects of life in the British colony lie in the sense of solidarity and cultural integrity provided by Mr Maxted's 'entertainments committee' whose nightly pro- gramme of lectures, theatre plays and concert parties sustain Jim's curiosity and vitality throughout the first year spent in captivity.

By opting for a third-person narrative that renders the story exclusively through the point of view of his former Shanghai self, Ballard turns the whole novel into a *Bildungsroman* that retraces Jim's development from childhood to maturity through a double process of initiation and individuation, one which revolves primarily around his changing sense of self as well as his relationship with other human beings. Like Ballard's earlier novels, *Empire of the Sun* is divided into a series of short chapters of approximately ten pages, each of which frames a particular stage or 'meaningful crisis' in Jim's mental development. What undoubtedly started as a convention of popular, serialized science fiction has become a characteristic feature of Ballard's narratives, which, as we have seen, tend to centre on a single character's interior journey through a complex and ambiguous process of spiritual transformation followed by the prospect of a future regeneration and its symbolic extension to the whole of mankind. Most prominent among the formative stages of Jim's experience of the war is a succession of 'mirror scenes' tracing a pattern of disembodiment and alienation leading to moments of self-awareness and reintegration. The first of these occurs shortly before Jim's internment in Lunghua camp when the child, facing the 'star-like image of himself' in a broken mirror, realizes that 'pieces of himself seemed to fly across the room, scattered through the empty house' (*ES* 63). After the war has radically shattered his identity and demolished his settled values and notions of life, Jim – who later becomes aware that 'parts of his mind and body frequently separated themselves from each other' – remarks that 'a strange doubling of reality' has taken place in the prison camp, 'as if everything that had happened to him since the war was occurring within a mirror' (*ES*, 112, 103). Having decided that 'it was his mirror self who felt hungry, and who thought about food all the time', Jim no longer feels sorry for himself and becomes even more determined to endure the hardships of the prison camp.

The theme of the divided self is once again re-enacted in Jim's interaction with two other major characters in the novel, who embody two basic attitudes to life: one amoral and ruthlessly optimistic (Basie) and one which is, instead, based on compassion and self-sacrifice (Dr Ransom). Basie, an American merchant seaman, and a shameless and unprincipled individual with a 'bland, unmarked face from which all the copious experiences of his life had been cleverly erased' (*ES* 94), represents more than just the negative aspects of life in the prison camp. He gives Jim (who was previously called Jamie) 'a new name for a new life' (*ES* 95) and, even more importantly, teaches him basic survival skills. For Jim, who lost his parents in the chaos of the Japanese invasion and was subsequently detained in another civilian camp (this is Ballard's most significant departure from the 'true' story of his Shanghai childhood), Dr Ransom represents the moral and cultural authority that had shaped his former self until the war began. Even though Ransom – whose name suggests both the possibility of rescue and the price that has to be paid to achieve this deliverance – seems to resent the child 'for revealing an obvious truth about the war, that people were only too able to adapt to it' (*ES* 208), his friendship with Jim nevertheless remains one of the few elements of psychological stability in the camp.

As Jim's identity wavers between these two extremes – which stand for physical and spiritual survival respectively – his experience of life in Lunghua camp is often expressed in a surreal and visionary fashion mixing reality and dream, history and myth. His attempts to make sense of the incomprehensible logic of the war in imaginative terms give Ballard an opportunity to create some memorable Surrealist-inspired imagery, such as the child's description of a Chinese burial tumulus at the centre of a sugar-cane field as 'rotting coffins projected from the loose earth like a chest of drawers' (*ES* 29). Jim's feeling that he is 'awake and asleep at the same time, dreaming of the war and yet dreamed of by the war' (*ES* 260) also accounts for other visionary passages which are often linked with his dreams of flight as well as with his fascination with both American and Japanese aircraft, which he sees as emissaries of light and redemption. More specifically, Jim's unquestioning admiration for the Japanese kamikaze pilots – whose contempt for death relates to his own tendency to welcome 'the likelihood of his own death' about which he has thought 'in a clandestine way' since his arrival at the prison camp (*ES* 194) – enables him to transcend his inner conflicts through the power of his imagination. At the end of the novel, after his apparent 'resurrection' of a dead Japanese pilot whom he regards as his 'imaginary twin' (*ES* 337), Jim even sees himself as the Saviour of the millions of people who have died during the war. This particular episode points back to a similar dream fantasy of global regeneration related in 'The Dead Time', a short story which Ballard published as early as 1977 in Emma Tennant's literary magazine *Bananas*. In Ballard's story, a young man of 20 who has just been released from the camp a week after the Japanese capitulation is forced to drive a truck loaded with dead bodies to a Shanghai cemetery. The narrator later identifies with the corpses and, out of a sense of loyalty to the dead, pledges himself to revitalize and repopulate the land, becoming 'the instrument of the new order which [he] had been delegated by them to bring to the world' (*MNF* 160).

The Day of Creation (1987) swerves away from the autobiographical strain of *Empire of the Sun* and back again to one of Ballard's most cherished genres: the dream-allegory. Superficially speaking, *The Day of Creation* may be seen as the diametrical opposite of *The Drought*. Taking place in the arid landscapes of a rundown central African republic, the novel gravitates round the sudden appearance of a river discovered by Dr Mallory, a physician attached to the World Health Organization. The allegorical dimension of the story emerges with Mallory's subsequent quest for the river's source in the company of a 12-year-old native girl called Noon. Mallory's quest gradually comes to represent a journey into his unconscious self, as well as a (failed) attempt to revive a physical and spiritual wasteland.

Noon is significantly more complex than Ballard's previous female characters. Although she exists primarily as an inverted reflection of Mallory's own spiritual transformation (her final disappearance coincides with that of the river, leaving Mallory with the feeling that he might have invented her to sustain himself in his quest for the river's sources), she is also endowed with a will and a personality of her own. At the outset of the story, Noon is depicted as a mute, physically and mentally bruised child whose graceful and stylized gestures seem to be 'endlessly rehearsing the elements of a richer and more elegant life' (*DC* 89). The young girl, who has enrolled herself in the local guerrilla unit, gradually develops into a powerful and mature woman whose deeper motives remain unreadable to Mallory till the end of the novel. Noon's spiritual and cultural metamorphosis truly begins with her discovery of a cheap prewar Hollywood melodrama describing the adventures of a female Tarzan played by 'a statuesque Texan blonde'. Although it is packed with hackneyed images conveying a caricature of the West's colonialist view of Africa, the old movie, far from imposing restraints on the child's imagination, provides her with 'the first dream of herself' (*DC* 177) as the paradoxical archetype of a fake African warrior queen.

Throughout the novel, it remains unclear, at least in Mallory's mind, whether the river is real or merely a literalized figment of his imagination. The theme of illusion versus reality is once more closely related to Ballard's concern with postindustrial societies and the new communication technologies, here represented by Professor Sanger and Mr Pal, producers of dubious nature films in which the African wildlife is sentimentalized into cliché-ridden 'soap documentaries' (*DC* 57). Ironically, however, Mallory – who until then had condemned Sanger's assumption that 'television's flattering revision of nature was an act of creation as significant as the original invention of this great river' – eventually remembers his journey to the river's source in terms of Sanger's imaginary travelogue, which 'alone seems to give meaning to all that took place' (*DC* 159, 286).

This final recognition of the demise of the real is an essential element of *The Kindness of Women* (1991), which, in addition to providing the reader with a series of biographical clues as to how and when some of Ballard's most powerful obsessions began to emerge, also presents a consciously devised aesthetic of the postindustrial landscape generated by memories of and a return visit to wartime Shanghai. The novel ends with Jim's uneasy response to the re-creation in Shepperton studios of wartime Shanghai for Steven Spielberg's 1987 film version of the now immensely popular *Empire of the Sun*. Now that his life (and, in a certain sense, Ballard's work) has 'come full circle' (*KW* 328), Jim cannot help being aware of the discrepancy between himself and his dream-like former Lunghua self, and concludes that 'this is the right way to go back to Shanghai, inside a film' (*KW* 333), thereby echoing his own comments, earlier in the novel, that 'Shanghai, too, had been a media city, perhaps the first of all, purpose-built by the West as a test-metropolis of the future'. 'London in the 1960s', he adds, 'had been the second, with the same confusions of image and reality, the same overheating' (*KW* 233). Jim's recognition of the blurring of boundaries between the real and its medium is once again reminiscent of Jean Baudrillard's famous dictum on the nature of reality in an image-saturated postindustrial world, the real becoming 'not only what can be reproduced, *but that which is always already reproduced*'.[1] In the era of the 'simulacrum', fiction has taken the place of reality as such, and what the visionary self tends to perceive as the 'authentic' is always already a dubious copy of a no longer recoverable original. Jim's uneasiness with the phenomenal, heavily mediatized success brought about by Spielberg's movie signals the final vengeance of the mass-media machine onto one of its most dedicated critical commentators. (Ironically enough, Jim's criticism of the war newsreels, one of the conceptual cruxes of the novel, was significantly downplayed in the film version.)

Ballard's treatment of media culture, however, is not overly critical, as it seeks to convey the many fascinations and dangers the new media hold for both Jim's generation and our own. Using a technique which has become typical of his 'novels of ideas', Ballard likes to confront contradictory beliefs – including his own conflicting views about contemporary society – by dramatizing them in dialectical conversations between his characters. Arguing with his friend Dick Sutherland, a psychologist won over by the glamorous logic of popular television, about the future of media culture, Jim claims: 'Nothing is seen in context anymore. Switch on your TV set, Dick, and you'll find a murdered prime minister, a child eating a candy bar, Marilyn lifting her skirt – what sort of a scenario is the mind quietly stitching together?' (*KW* 237). Jim's misgivings about the decontextualized, free-floating images of current media practice and its effects on the minds of individuals raised in front of a television draws upon the central thematic and structural concerns underlying the paratactic synopses of *The Atrocity Exhibition*. For Jim, the mind's capacity to yoke together apparently distinct and unrelated electronic images into an endless number of imaginary narratives (some of which may prove more harmful than others) is an essential key to the understanding of the mechanisms of late contemporary consciousness. Any attempt at a global reading of the fractured logic of a media landscape characterized by an ever-increasing fragmentation of representation is doomed to failure. In view of the increasing mechanization of culture and its transformation by the media industry (of which Ballard's experimental fiction may appear as both a symptom and a critique), the means of interpreting reality seem to have slipped from the hands of psychologists and sociologists into those of admen, film critics ('in the future', Jim concludes, 'one will need to be a film critic to make sense of anything', KW 237) or, arguably, semioticians such as Baudrillard or Ballard himself. The more specific failure of conventional, Freudian-inspired psychology to come to terms with a free flow of images subsuming traditional boundaries between the latent and the manifest is suggested by Dick Sutherland's transformation from a brilliant Cambridge academic into 'the reluctant fugleman of popular psychology, feeding news of the latest breakthroughs to his coterie of TV producers' (KW 235).

While the first part of the novel returns us to Jim's Shanghai childhood, its central section recounts his return to England as a young medical student at Cambridge, his short-lived career in the RAF and, finally, his married life which is shattered by his wife's accidental death. What follows is an account of the peculiar logic of sex, drugs and violence of the 1960s and, more specifically, of Jim's attempts to heal his damaged psyche, helped by the kindness and affection of a number of women-friends and lovers. As suggested above, *The Kindness of Women* contains a variety of semi-autobiographical keys to the interpretation of the major themes and motifs of Ballard's oeuvre. One chapter, for instance, deals with an exhibition of sculptures made from wrecked automobiles which was actually staged by Ballard at the London New Arts Laboratory in 1970. Jim explains that the crashed car, which 'summed up so many of [his] obsessions at the time', was a 'repository of the most powerful and engaged emotions, a potent symbol in the new logic of violence and sensation that ruled our lives' (KW 221). In his catalogue notes, he writes what reads like a summary of the symptomatological theories developed in *The Atrocity Exhibition*:

> The marriage of reason and nightmare which dominates the 1960s has given birth to an ever more ambiguous world. Across the communications landscape stride the spectres of sinister technologies and the dreams that money can buy. Thermonuclear weapons systems and soft-drink commercials coexist in an uneasy realm ruled by advertising and pseudo-events, science and pornography. The death of feeling and emotion has at last left us free to pursue our

own psychopathologies as a game...'Crashed Cars' illustrates the pandemic cataclysm that kills hundreds of thousands of people each year and injures millions, but is a source of endless entertainment on our film and television screens. (KW 221–2)

Here, as elsewhere, Ballard seems at his best when working within the tradition of polemical Happenings that began to flourish in the years that preceded his debut as a professional writer. Characteristically seizing on the contradiction between the glamorous, entertainment-oriented medium of the communication landscape and its actual, lethal and destructive message, Ballard uses the car crash as a powerful metaphor for what he sees as the peculiar dream of violence and desire embodied by the sixties, a vision which emphasizes the dual character of the new media technology as both the destroyer and potential restorer of feeling and emotion. Indeed, the 'ecology of violence' emblematized by the crashed car exhibition may reflect the 'numbing brutality' of the sixties; it also appears as a means of coming to terms with the violence and sensation of the age and of restoring 'a lost compassion' (KW 216). If The Kindness of Women as a whole seeks to account for the reification of human relationships and the loss of feeling and emotion, then the second half of the novel is precisely about the survival of affect in the author's middle years. In many respects, the semi-autobiographical credibility and the uncompromising honesty which emanates from Ballard's account of Jim's 'craze years' make it an even more thought-provoking and disturbing book than the 'library of extreme metaphors' (KW 342) catalogued in The Atrocity Exhibition and Crash.

Because of the many links they create between Jim's past experiences and his development as a person and artist, Empire of the Sun and The Kindness of Women are liable to be interpreted as self-conscious attempts to reveal the origins of some of Ballard's fictional obsessions. Jim's memories of his Shanghai childhood, in particular, conjure up a number of 'primal scenes' evoking what were later to become the hallmarks of Ballard's novels and short stories.[2] The empty villas, drained swimming pools, abandoned airfields, the media, the dreams of flight, the sun and light imagery which provide an almost inescapable background to many of his writings are all there, waiting to be decoded retrospectively in the light of the author's autobiographical experience. Lastly, the sense of global entropic devolution which pervades the early science fiction stories is epitomized by Jim's vision of the impersonal energy of the Nagasaki bomb as 'a premonition of his death, the sight of his small soul joining the larger soul of the dying world' (ES 267).

The temptation to read Ballard's oeuvre through the lens of his Shanghai childhood has led some critics to construct larger narratives that encompass the whole of his career. Reflecting on Jim's loss of faith in the authority of family and culture and his fascination with 'the imagery of technology of death that he finds in American war machinery and films',[3] Dennis Foster, for instance, argues that 'Crash gives some idea of what Jim will become, the maker of television commercials obsessed with the relations among technology and identity and death'.[4] The exact nature of the interaction of autobiographical and fictional material in The Kindness of Women has been discussed by Ballard himself who, in a recent interview, declared that his novel was not an autobiographical novel in the strict sense, but the story of a life 'seen through the mirror of the fiction prompted by that life'.[5] The fact that Ballard's parents and children are almost entirely left out of his 'autobiographical' novels suggests that his main concern is not to offer an objective and exhaustive account of his past experiences, but to dramatize his quest for his own childhood self, which was stolen from him – or, at least 'postponed' (KW 342) – by the war. Such concerns tie in with Dr Yasuda's remark, in 'The Terminal Beach', that 'every parent in the world mourns the lost sons and daughters of their past childhood' (BSS 262). By exploring a spectrum of unresolved conflicts and solitary mind games that date back to the author's childhood, The Kindness of Women evidently suggests that one cannot escape the burden of one's psychic past. Perhaps more importantly, however, it also brings an end to the process of mourning initiated by Jim's internment in Lunghua camp and offers the prospect of new psychological and aesthetic tactics that lie beyond the 'desperate stratagems' of the 'craze years' (KW 342).

9

More News from the Near Future

The American critic Nicholas Zurbrugg has interpreted the intellectual honesty and emotional credibility which pervades Ballard's autobiographical novels as a sign of his recovery from 'his erstwhile panic mentality'.[1] By making 'a clean break with the earlier, more pessimistic... stories', he writes, '*The Kindness of Women* suggests that Ballard is now best described as one of the great contemporary *ex-dystopians*'.[2] Zurbrugg's analysis is typical of an all too common tendency to settle for an understanding of Ballard's recent fiction as a breakaway from the lurid and tormented psychopathological paradigms of *The Atrocity Exhibition* in favour of a redeeming 'catharsis'.[3] There are a number of things wrong with this claim. The first is that it reduces Ballard's career to a process of gradual enlightenment in which the author allegedly grows out of his radical and sensationalist prose into a more affirmative, and one supposes more 'responsible' and 'mature', approach to contemporary culture. Such an interpretation appears all the more questionable since the aesthetic and political premises of Ballard's early fiction have continued to run through the later novels in a way that allows the reader to retroactively 'revisit' and reinvent them in the light of subsequent formal and thematic modulations. The second, and more important, objection that can be raised against Zurbrugg's argument is that Ballard's fiction was never in the least characterized by a 'panic mentality'. On the contrary, even Ballard's most apocalyptic stories convey a peaceful sense of acceptance of the individual's devolutionary descent into a state of timeless, inorganic stasis that is anything but desperate. As for that most sensational dystopian speculation known as the 'death of affect', its main consequence is precisely to prevent Ballard's characters from experiencing anything remotely associated with such feelings as fear or anxiety.

Ballard's thirteenth novel, *Rushing to Paradise* (1994), suggests, if need be, that his interest in extremisms of all kinds has not yet begun to falter. The motif of the marooned individual suddenly severed from civilization and capable of reverting to various forms of primitive savagery once again provides the focal point for Ballard's novel, which is concerned with the latent and manifest motives of Dr Barbara Rafferty, the charismatic leader of a community of radical environmentalists overrunning the deserted Pacific atoll of Saint-Esprit. After their arrival on the main island, it soon becomes apparent that all the members of the expedition have different reasons for embracing the cause of the albatross threatened by a crowd of French soldiers and engineers who have recently returned to the island to build an airstrip. Among them is 16-year-old Neil Dempsey, who is fascinated by the atoll's nuclear testing-ground, which he sees as a concrete manifestation of his dreams of nuclear death. For Neil (who was originally drawn to the island because it embodied 'a demonstration model of Armageddon, a dream of war and death that lay beyond the reach of any moratorium', *RP* 16), nuclear weapons hold the key to a transfiguring, rather than a destructive, experience. The ship's helmsman, Kimo, is a former sergeant in the Honolulu police who, in joining the protest raid against the French authorities, nurses the secret hope of building an independent Hawaiian kingdom. As for 'Dr Barbara' herself, it turns out that her intention is not to save the albatross but to transform Saint Esprit into a breeding sanctuary for women, whom she comes to consider as the real endangered species. Her purpose then becomes to turn the island colony into 'a sanctuary for all [the women's] threatened strengths, their fire, rage and cruelty' (*RP* 171). Far from becoming a space in which women can de-domesticate themselves and recover their lost dignity, Dr Barbara's matriarchal regime soon turns out to be a means for her to satisfy her own grim obsessions. Her cruel, paranoid and self-interested behaviour gradually supplants her new agenda and eventually leads her to folly and murder.

Like the 'psychic landscapes' of Ballard's early disaster novels, the island becomes both a catalyst and a symbolic extension of Dr Barbara's unstated motives. More specifically, the island-based narrative of *Rushing to Paradise* bears echoes of Ballard's previous inverted 'robinsonnade' in *Concrete Island* as well as of H. G. Wells's *The Island of Dr Moreau* (1896), another devolutionary story dealing with the sinister consequences of an enlightened project hijacked by a utopian obsession. The ambivalent energies that motivate Dr Barbara's 'cruel and generous heart' (*RP* 239) can be interpreted as an allegorical illustration of how the affirmative powers of vision are likely to be engulfed by the alarming dynamics of fanaticism. Still, the possibility of reading Ballard's novel as a didactic fable is precluded by the author's ambiguous relationship with his protagonist, which seems characterized by a mixture of admiration and repulsion. As Ballard himself has pointed out, Dr Barbara represents much more than the 'enchantress figure'[4] dominating his earlier works. She is, he comments, 'an immensely powerful, strong-willed woman who has all the ancient, ancestral power of women as creators, as controllers, as enchanters of men, as crones, as mothers – all those archetypal female images, which have so terrified and inspired men through the ages, are incarnated in a small way in this character'.[5]

Most of the story is told through the eyes of Neil Dempsey, who finds himself drawn to Dr Barbara's sexual magnetism and becomes 'determined at whatever cost to protect her from reality' (*RP* 18). Almost until the very end, the boy remains faithful to Dr Barbara's obsessive crusade, nourished by the timeless uterine depths of the Pacific atoll and paradoxically sustained by his fascination with the prospect of global nuclear destruction. Characteristically, the possibility of global annihilation – which explicitly parallels Dr Barbara's own apocalyptic schemes – is placed in the context of a pervasive feeling that Ballard's characters live in an eternal present which blunts their sense of narrative and historical connection. Neil's feeling, later in the story, that 'a collective amnesia of the future [has] settled over the sanctuary' (*RP* 211) points to the diminished awareness of linear time which prevails on the island of Saint-Esprit and, indeed, in most of Ballard's fictional worlds. Ballard's vision of late-twentieth-century society is, once again, consistently post-cultural and post-historical – 'increasingly', he writes elsewhere, 'our concepts of the past, present, and future are being forced to revise themselves. Just as the past itself, in social and psychological terms, became a casualty of Hiroshima' and 'the future is ceasing to exist, devoured by the all-voracious present' (*R/S* 97). Ballard's claim that 'we have annexed the future into our own present, as merely one of those manifold alternatives open to us' (*R/S* 97) joins with what some poststructuralist theorists, such as Fredric Jameson, have defined as the 'weakening of historicity' in the postmodern era.[6] In an essay devoted to nuclear weapons and their impact on current power relations and literary agendas, another polemical commentator on contemporary culture, the novelist Martin Amis, holds a similar view, arguing that the threat of global annihilation has radically upset traditional notions of time. 'An infinite fall', he writes, 'underl[ying] the usual – indeed traditional – presentiments of decline' has resulted in a sense that 'the past and the future, equally threatened, equally cheapened, now huddle in the present'.[7]

On a more practical, though no less polemical, level, there is no doubt that the story implicitly refers to real life events, and it is hard not to read *Rushing to Paradise* without being reminded of the French nuclear test island of Mururoa, to which the Greenpeace ship *Rainbow Warrior* was about to sail when it was sunk in Auckland Harbour in July 1985. The fact that Ballard's novel was published roughly a year before Jacques Chirac's decision to resume nuclear testing on Mururoa adds a premonitory touch to the satirical strain of Ballard's novel. As is often the case in Ballard's fiction, however, the specific 'issue' which constitutes the starting point of the story is gradually stifled by the psychological depth and the allegorical dimension of the narrative, and it would therefore be a mistake to interpret the novel as (merely) a satire on extremist tendencies in either animal-rights activism or feminism. If *Rushing to Paradise* can certainly be read as a cautionary tale against political extremism in a general sense, it remains focused on a number of themes which have occupied Ballard since his early science fiction stories. These recurrent concerns include the dialectic of the latent and manifest meanings of our everyday lives, the potential of both natural and man-made landscapes for triggering unconscious drives, a refusal to indulge in sentimentalized images of nature, science and progress and, above all, the postulate that our personal and public commitments are always already preconditioned by our attempts to fictionalize the real.

The relatively contrived plotting and awkward dialogues make
Rushing to Paradise less than truly successful as either a
psychological study or a dystopian fantasy, even within the
bounds set by the author's leaning towards allegorical landscapes
and inner space poetics. Based as it is on a systematic – and
occasionally heavy-handed – examination of the dynamics of
obsession and the 'secret agendas'[8] lurking beneath any
programmatic political activity, Ballard's novel may also stand
accused of being too distinctively Ballardian to appeal to readers
acquainted with the author's earlier works. For all its flaws and
limitations, *Rushing to Paradise* nevertheless confirms, albeit in a
minor mode, Ballard's unique talent for dealing with small groups
of psychologically isolated individuals in extreme situations, a
concern which runs through almost all of his novels, from the
steamy jungles of *The Drowned World* to the suburban wasteland of
Concrete Island or Lunghua camp in *Empire of the Sun*.

Ballard has often spoken of science fiction as the only literary
mode capable of accommodating a range of social and political
issues all too often neglected by mainstream literature: 'All these
topics such as, "How do you run a society where a large
proportion of people will never work?" These are the sorts of
themes that classic SF treated' (*R/S* 124). The prospect of a life of
unlimited leisure and pure idleness is precisely the subject of
Vermilion Sands (1971), a collection of conceptually linked
dystopian parables taking place in a futuristic seaside resort
Ballard describes as 'an exotic suburb of [his] mind...celebrat[ing]
the neglected virtues of the glossy, lurid and bizarre' (*VS* 7). In
his Preface to the collection, Ballard places the timeless beaches
of this holiday paradise in the context of a worldwide movement
towards a leisure-oriented society:

> Where is Vermilion Sands? I suppose its spiritual home lies
> somewhere between Arizona and Ipanema Beach, but in recent
> years I have been delighted to see it popping up elsewhere – above
> all in sections of the 3,000-mile-long linear city that stretches from
> Gibraltar to Glyfada Beach along the northern shores of the
> Mediterranean, and where each summer Europe lies on its back in
> the sun. That posture, of course, is the hallmark of Vermilion Sands
> and, I hope, of the future – not merely that no-one has to work, but
> that work is the ultimate play, and play the ultimate work. (*VS* 7–8)

In spite of the attractiveness of its languorous atmosphere and countless exquisite amusements (which include various bizarre phenomena such as sonic sculptures, singing plants, sculptured clouds and 'bio-fabric' clothes adapting to the moods and personalities of their wearers), Ballard's seaside utopia has more than its share of frustrations and perversions, most of which appear as symptomatic of a culture which suffers from an excess of refinement and sophistication and has fallen into the bittersweet savour of decay. In this glamorous playground of the future peopled by forgotten movie queens, eccentric architects and other extravagant dilettantes, the only way out of permanent boredom seems to be to conjure up new social games and intrigues to enliven the world of eternal lethargy and 'beach fatigue' (*VS* 19). The general mood evoked by Ballard's stories is indeed that of a purposeless pantomime, an affectless void giving way to unpredictable acts of violence. Some of the most sordid side-effects of this future of utter boredom are illustrated by 'Say Goodbye to the Wind', in which the owner of a boutique specializing in bio-fabric fashions is nearly strangled by his own clothes, 'The Singing Statues', the story of a former movie star falling victim to extreme forms of narcissism, or 'The Thousand Dreams of Stellavista', in which one of the 'psychotropic houses' of the resort (which are trained to respond to their owners' mental characteristics) attempts to kill its occupants.

The stories of *Vermilion Sands* clearly prefigure the society of permanent leisure depicted in *Cocaine Nights* (1996), which confirms Ballard's view of science fiction as an ideal medium for technological and sociological extrapolation; a vision claimed by some critics as being the privilege of the more respectable-sounding genre called 'speculative fiction'. The setting is the Spanish resort of Estrella de Mar, an idyllic community peopled by British residents enjoying constant and organized sporting and cultural activity – a thriving arts community, film clubs, amateur theatre companies and choral societies make it an unlikely cross between Greenwich Village and the average Mediterranean holiday resort. On a strictly visual level, the seaside landscapes of Estrella de Mar provide Ballard with an opportunity to create some haunting visions of gilded dunes, deserted beaches, abandoned villas and empty swimming pools which have become recognizable trademarks of his fiction since the early short stories of *The Voices of Time* and *The Terminal Beach*. One of the most fascinating features of the novel derives from Ballard's celebration of what Baudrillard would probably describe as the 'obscene surfaces' of a make-believe world based on the culture of the pastiche and the 'hyperreal'. With its mock-Roman architecture, Disneyland-like theme villages, 'cubist apartments' (*CN* 34), 'filling-stations disguised as cathedrals' and even a larger-than-life replica of the White House owned by an Arab oil prince, Ballard's Costa Brava emerges as 'a zone as depthless as a property developer's brochure' (*CN* 16). It is a place where 'the future [has] come ashore', dominated by an architecture 'dedicated to the abolition of time' and plunging the numbed brains of its occupants into 'a special kind of willed limbo':

> The memory-erasing white architecture; the enforced leisure that fossilized the nervous system; the almost Africanized aspect, but a North Africa invented by someone who had never visited the Maghreb; the apparent absence of any social structure; the timelessness of a world beyond boredom, with no past, no future and a diminishing present. Perhaps this was what a leisure-dominated future should resemble? Nothing could ever happen in this affectless realm, where entropic drift calmed the surfaces of a thousand swimming pools. (*CN* 34–5)

The plot of Ballard's novel superficially resembles that of a classic murder mystery – but one which follows the lurid associational and intertextual logic of a David Lynch movie. The narrator, Charles Prentice, a travel writer who defines himself as a 'professional tourist' (*CN* 9), arrives at Estrella de Mar to discover that his younger brother Frank, manager of the booming Club Nautico – one of the most exclusive sports complexes in the area – has been charged with starting the fire that killed five people during a party attended by local residents. The novel centres on his attempts to understand the 'deviant logic' (*CN* 78) which prompts his brother to plead guilty, though not even the police believe him capable of the crime. Interpreting his brother's plea of guilty as 'part of some bizarre game he [is] playing against himself' and an unconscious attempt to initiate him into the 'inner life' of Estrella de Mar, Charles gradually begins to feel at home at the Club Nautico and even experiences 'a curious complicity' in the crime he is trying to solve (*CN* 29, 160, 79).

But the real protagonist of the novel is the tennis trainer Bobby Crawford, whose avowed ambition is to free the residents of Estrella de Mar from their mind-deadening habits and return them to 'their true selves' (*CN* 240). In order to achieve his goal, Crawford proceeds to encourage wayward forms of violence and sexuality through which he sets out to 'grace their lives with the possibilities of being sinful and immoral' (*CN* 179). His evangelical fervour and sexual charisma gradually enable him to assert his ascendancy over the whole resort. Responding to Crawford's influence, the residents at Estrella de Mar begin to take part in an elaborate and dangerous 'bureaucracy of crime' (*CN* 257) whose ultimate purpose is to quicken the emotional life of its participants and create a strong sense of community among them. Crawford's symbolic role as a messiah figure is made clear by a reference to Pasolini's film *Theorem* (1969), another politico-sexual allegory gravitating round the spiritual transfiguration of a slumbering community by a mysterious stranger. In the larger context of Ballard's oeuvre, Crawford emerges as a somewhat sinister reincarnation of the Pied Piper figure embodied by Blake in *The Unlimited Dream Company*. Charles Prentice's remark that he has 'turned the Costasol residents into children, filling their lives with adult toys and inviting them out to play' (*CN* 309), points to his status as a paradoxical synthesis of innocence and corruption. Crawford – who is described as a 'bruised and boyish visionary' with a 'dazed schoolboy grin' and 'innocent and visionary eyes' (*CN* 263, 40, 259) – enacts what the narrator of *Rushing to Paradise* terms 'the revenge of a perpetual child' (*RP* 155) tormented by painful memories of unresolved family anxieties, crushed by the social pressures of an over-rationalized society and longing to return to 'a realm of aroused emotions and woken dreams' (*CN* 276).

Politically speaking, what is at stake in Ballard's eventless future is the possibility of envisaging an alternative economy of the social whole in which deviance becomes 'a commodity under jealous guard' (*CN* 135), at least in the context of a community threatened by the prospect of an overkill of stability and monotony. The narrator's observation that the sense of 'total security' prevailing at Estrella de Mar amounts to 'a disease of deprivation' (*CN* 293) can be usefully related to the notion of 'unproductive expenditure' championed by French writer Georges Bataille. In Bataille's theories, as in Ballard's fiction, this general principle of social waste – which transgresses the basic processes of production and consumption necessary for the survival of any given society – includes not only art, games and leisure but also wars, religious cults, ritual sacrifice and perverse (i.e. non-genital) sexuality. In *Cocaine Nights*, however, such 'unproductive' activities can no longer be considered as an alternative to the homogenizing and commodifying processes of productive activity. They exist in a social, moral and political void; an artificial and apparently single-class society which seems peopled exclusively by a privileged group of well-to-do professionals flanked by prosperous real-estate salesmen, architects and hotel managers. In the absence of any significant social and economic tension, it soon becomes apparent that the netherworld of drugs, illicit sex and gratuitous crime (ranging from petty thefts to murder and rape) that lurks beneath the civilized surface of the seaside resort results from a more general need to resharpen the sensibilities of all the residents and, ultimately, set the terms for 'the last carnival blaze' (*CN* 160) that will sooner or later seal the fate of Crawford's utopia.

Inscribed in the logic of contraries, as well as in the dialectics of sacrifice and redemption, *Cocaine Nights* signals the advent of the 'psychopath as saint' (*CN* 280), the purveyor of a messianic sexuality which ties in with Ballard's conviction that 'the psychopathic should be preserved as a nature reserve, a last refuge for a certain kind of human freedom' in a world he perceives as an increasingly uniform and conformist space reflecting a worldwide 'suburbanization of the soul'.[9] One suspects that Ballard is sympathetic to Crawford's cause and regards his character as another avatar of the 'unlimited dreamer' called for as a rescuing and communifying force at a time when the toppling of binding rules for morality has created simultaneously a desire for alternative truths and a need for new forms of guilt and subversive behaviour. In this respect, Ballard's novel remains faithful to his commitment to a form of fiction writing that not only undermines the narrative and characterological categories of the 'realist' novel, but also sets out to diagnose the changing parameters of human identity and subjectivity in an essentially post-humanist world.

10

Reflections in Place of a Conclusion

As suggested in the preceding chapters, one way of appraising J. G. Ballard's unique position in the history of contemporary literature is to say that his fiction seeks to challenge nothing less than the psychic and material parameters by which we attempt to regulate our everyday lives and understand the nature of reality and of our own aspirations and fantasies. Rejecting traditional notions concerning the necessary ascendancy of the rational mind, Ballard's view of modern life emphasizes the process by which society enters the individual and establishes a fundamental separation between reason and impulse, thereby negating the all-pervading force of unconscious desire which, as we have seen, stands as both the possibility of self-fulfilment and the danger of self-annihilation. This particular feature of his fiction ties in with his vision of contemporary society as based on a set of values that entail the loss of instinctual freedom in the name of a 'reality principle' that has taken the form of delayed satisfaction, safer planning and greater efficiency in all fields of modern life.

That Ballard's catastrophe scenarios almost invariably take place within societies which have reached a high level of social welfare and technological sophistication is indicative of his concern with how violence and brutality can be unleashed by a freedom- and progress-oriented society. Another useful parallel can be drawn here between Ballard's social critique and the opening proposition of Theodor Adorno and Max Horkheimer's *Dialectic of Enlightenment*: 'In the most general sense of progressive thought, the Enlightenment has always aimed at liberating men from fear and establishing their sovereignty. Yet the fully enlightened earth radiates disaster triumphant'.[1] What Adorno and Horkheimer are warning against is that the concept of reason upheld by Enlightenment thinking (as well as by its practical extension into the Industrial Revolution and modern technologies) as the supreme agent of freedom and progress for all mankind bears the seeds of a totalizing, and potentially totalitarian, view of the common good that may lead to the psychological confinement of the individual. Such utopian visions of unity and stability, Ballard's fiction suggests, spur the desire for deviance and change: the mysterious subliminal compulsions which dominate the lives of his characters emerge as a symptom of our incapacity to subdue the flow of our unconscious drives and conform to various forms of social and political restrictions; as such, they enact the return of the socially and culturally repressed. Seen from this angle, Ballard joins a line of modern writers who, from Joseph Conrad to William Golding and beyond, have spoken eloquently of the actual or latent brutalities of modern history in a way that emphasizes that magnetizing obscurity of the prerational mind which society seeks to dominate for better or worse.

Ballard is a writer who has gone through a remarkable number of formal and conceptual transformations, but the guiding thread in his work seems to be an interest in the emergence of modern media technology within the domain of the aesthetic. According to Ballard, the mass media have also brought significant changes to the very function and methods of literature – hence his conception of science fiction as 'a response to science and technology as perceived by the inhabitants of the consumer goods society [which] recognises that the role of the writer today has totally changed – he is now merely one of a huge army of people filling the environment with fictions of every kind' (R/S 99). When not considered over-literally, Ballard's radical scepticism can be elucidated and justified in the light of the assumption that any attempt to account for an innocent or unmediated version of the 'real' is an act of bad faith. By providing a model for the modes of consciousness that are being produced by the new information technologies, Ballard shows the way to an aesthetic that might be capable of making statements about its political and social backgrounds while acknowledging the historicity of its own conditions of production. Central to this aesthetic is the assumption that the experience of information technology – with its infinite network of interconnections, analogies and simulacra – has altered our understanding of the workings of society as a whole, at the same time as undermining the notion of a thinking subject that is autonomous and coherent unto itself. For Ballard's characters, in many ways, reality itself becomes whatever is fabricated by their desires; the human mind becoming – in McLuhanite terms – the 'medium' in which the real forms and transforms itself, refusing to be caught in 'those muffling layers of blood and bones, reflex and convention'.[2]

More generally, Ballard's fiction remains torn between two contradictory impulses: that of celebrating the unfettered urges of the libidinal self, and that of doing justice to a society in which the tension between ego and id, self and world seems regulated by the glamorous and seamless surfaces of the mass media. Ballard's ambivalent position towards the media machine is perhaps best understood in the light of McLuhan's description of his strategies of apprehension of contemporary culture in *The Mechanical Bride*. Commenting on Edgar Allen Poe's 'A Descent into the Maelstrom', McLuhan writes:

> Poe's sailor saved himself by studying the action of the whirlpool and by cooperating with it. The present book likewise makes few attempts to attack the considerable currents and pressures set up around us today by the mechanical agencies of the press, radio, movies, and advertising. It does attempt to set the reader at the center of the revolving picture created by these affairs where he may observe the action that is in progress and in which everybody is involved. From the analysis of that action, it is hoped, many individual strategies may suggest themselves.[3]

Ballard's fiction suggests an important way of coping with this situation in its renewed recourse to patterns of cooperation and conflict that explore the internal contradictions of contemporary culture and attempt to pinpoint them as the locus of the potential reconciliation of self and world. To quote from an early article on the art of Salvador Dali, at least part of the uneasiness generated by Ballard's fiction derives from its attempt not only to depict 'the psychic crisis that produced this glaucous paradise' but also 'to document the uneasy pleasures of living within it' (*UGM* 91).

Throughout his career, Ballard has become increasingly attentive to the essential role played by the visual world and the new communication technologies in triggering violent and radical changes within the individual. In one of his most provocative statements to date, Ballard has argued that, since the subliminal effects of TV and video culture have made our 'imaginative demands for greater sexual freedom' more urgent than ever, 'there should be more sex and violence on television, not less'. 'Both', he continues, 'are powerful catalysts of social change, at a time when change is desperately needed' (*UGM* 5). Ballard's call for more sex and violence on TV, along with a number of other equally controversial statements made over the last thirty years, is clearly in keeping with some of the dystopian precepts which, since *The Atrocity Exhibition*, have inspired and enriched his vision of contemporary culture. Unfortunately, it is also typical of a line of theoretical speculation whose radical and progressive premises are liable to culminate in sheer idealism, mainly because they fail to truly account for the social and cultural specifics of our time. What is indeed conspicuously absent from Ballard's argument is a concern with the material conditions of production and consumption of mass-media artefacts. Even though one may understand, and even sympathize with, Ballard's fascination with the numinous energies of unconscious desire, it is less easy to follow him when he argues that a thirty-second ad for call-girls on a private American TV channel ranks with *Blue Velvet* and *The Hitcher* as 'one of the most interesting films of today' (*UGM* 5). More generally, Ballard's postulate that televised sex and violence can promote social emancipation seems to ignore the blatant mercantilism of media culture, which – dominated as it is by corporate interests and conservative ideology – has arguably little to offer in terms of a genuinely subversive libidinal investment and little to do with any protopolitical prospects of real or fantasized social improvements. In fact, one could argue exactly the opposite and conclude that all the consumers of these mass-cultural artefacts will ever be capable of is what the market demands of them.

One is reminded here of Charles Prentice's sceptical responses to Bobby Crawford's proselytism in *Cocaine Nights*, which raise a number of similar, commonsensical objections to the redeeming power of transgressive behaviour and its supposed capacity to 'quicken the nervous system and jump the synapses deadened by leisure and inaction' (*CN* 180). In what resembles an attempt to put Ballard's theories to the test of his readers' willingness to accept the peculiar logic of his fiction on its own terms, Prentice comments: 'Does one follow the other? I don't believe it. If someone burgles my house, shoots the dog and rapes the maid my reaction isn't to open an art gallery' (*CN* 181).

If Ballard's immodest proposals allegedly have little to offer in terms of practical alternatives to what he sees as the social and political lethargy of our postindustrial societies, they have nevertheless shown themselves ready to grapple with a number of aspects of contemporary society left unconsidered by most 'mainstream' contemporary novelists in Britain. Indeed, if Ballard often tends to deny the self any direct access to a reality 'uncontaminated' by the play of images and 'simulacra' that dominates the era of media reproduction, his best fiction does not by any means seek to evade 'real' forms of social and cultural experience. His more recent novels, in particular, have tended to elaborate on the effects of the mass media on specific issues such as the American Dream (*Hello America*), suburban violence (*Running Wild*), World War II (*Empire of the Sun*), the Third World economy (*The Day of Creation*) and political extremism (*Rushing to Paradise*). Furthermore, and even though they may (deliberately) leave many intellectual and conceptual loose ends, Ballard's 'novels of ideas' generally succeed in providing the terms for a discussion of the global dynamics of modern societies and the workings of late-twentieth-century consciousness – one which is not grounded in the realist representation of social manners but in a patient investigation of the deepest reaches of the isolated self.

Far from presenting a nihilistic vision of the future, Ballard's unflinching visionary gifts – combined as they are with his now legendary brand of jaded scepticism – are sustained by a conviction that art should break through what Aldous Huxley called the 'doors of perception' and dismantle the screens that protect us from the richness of experience and revelation. Oscillating between the shock-tactics of *Crash* and *The Atrocity Exhibition* and the more conventional narrative strategies of his later novels, Ballard's fiction plays on the borders between the realms of realism and fantasy, the sublime and the perverse, the literal and the allegorical. Its capacity to create metaphors and depict experiences that are both regressive and transcendental, suicidal and life-giving, temporal and spiritual, makes his oeuvre one of the most unsettling, imaginative and uncompromisingly political fictional achievements of the latter half of this century. Thematically and formally, it holds an unusually wide range of reference to problems of psychology, morality, politics and social evolution; few other contemporary novelists have projected such powerful interrogations so deeply into the central preoccupations of our times.

Notes

CHAPTER 1. INTRODUCTION

1. Michael Moorcock's influential editorship played an important role in the careers of Ballard and other writers associated with the New Wave school. It should be noted, however, that Ted Carnell, Moorcock's predecessor as the editor of *New Worlds*, had already 'discovered' Ballard (and published his first short story, 'Escapement') as early as 1956.
2. For a detailed assessment of Ballard's ambiguous position between genre fiction and the mainstream, see R. Luckhurst, 'Petition, Repetition, and "Autobiography"': J. G. Ballard's *Empire of the Sun* and *The Kindness of Women*', *Contemporary Literature*, 35:4 (1994), 688–91.
3. Duncan Fallowell, 'Ballard in Bondage', *Books and Bookmen*, 21:6 (March 1976), 60.
4. Robert L. Platzner, 'The Metamorphic Vision of J. G. Ballard', *Essays in Literature*, 10:3 (1983), 210.
5. Platzner, 'The Metamorphic Vision', 215.
6. Platzner, 'The Metamorphic Vision', 216.

CHAPTER 2. THE NATURE OF THE CATASTROPHE

1. Quoted in Colin Greenland, *The Entropy Exhibition: Michael Moorcock and the British 'New Wave' in Science Fiction* (London: Routledge, 1983), 96.
2. Robert L. Platzner, 'The Metamorphic Vision of J. G. Ballard', *Essays in Literature*, 10:3 (1983), 209.
3. See chapter 3. Ransom's intimation that the face of his estranged wife Judith 'already carried the injuries of an appalling motor-car accident that would happen somewhere in the future' (*D.* 37) also prefigures the central metaphor of Ballard's novel *Crash*.

4. Another intriguing parallel can be made between Ballard's devolutionary landscapes and the earthworks of Robert Smithson, the American artist who died in 1973 after crashing into one of his own works in a private plane from which he was taking photographs. Smithson's famous 'Spiral Jetty' – a gigantic earth-sculpture located in Great Salt Lake, Utah – was meant to enact a similar devolutionary movement away from land into the water element, a process of geomorphic alteration enacting the dissolution of the individual into 'a unicellular beginning... mak[ing] one aware of protoplasmic solutions, the essential matter between the formed and the unformed' (*The Writings of Robert Smithson*, ed. Nancy Holt, New York University Press, New York, 1979, pp. 113–14). Smithson's essay 'The Artist as Site-Seer; or, A Dinotorphic Essay' (*Robert Smithson: Unearthed*, ed. Eugenie Tsai, Columbia University Press, New York, 1991, pp. 74–80) contains a number of references to and quotations from Ballard's early work.
5. See, in particular, Brian Aldiss's *An Age* (1967) and Michael Moorcock's Nebula Award winning novella *Behold the Man* (1967).
6. Another early story, 'Manhole 69', deals with scientific experiments in continual wakefulness resulting in an unbearable state of permanent awareness.
7. Jean-Paul Sartre, *Literary and Philosophical Essays*, trans. Annette Michelson (London: Rider, 1955), 79.
8. For a detailed discussion of the concept of entropy in contemporary American fiction, see chapters 4 and 7 in Tony Tanner's *City of Words: American Fiction 1950–1970* (London: Cape, 1971).
9. Thomas Pynchon, *Slow Learner* (London: Jonathan Cape, 1985), 83–4.
10. Pynchon, *Slow Learner*, 88.
11. See also Ballard's comment that his fiction is 'all about one person, all about one man coming to terms with various forms of isolation' (quoted in P. Brigg, *J. G. Ballard*, Starmont House, Mercer Island, WA, 1985, p. 37).
12. In an article published in a 1962 issue of *New Worlds*, Ballard argues for a kind of science fiction that reflects 'the sombre half-worlds one glimpses in the paintings of schizophrenics' (*UGM* 198). As is apparent in a recent piece entitled 'Project for a Glossary of the Twentieth Century', Ballard, in his critique of official attitudes towards madness and deviance, remains aware of the misleadingly glamorous appeal of schizophrenia in a society dominated by rationality. 'To the sane', he writes, '[schizophrenia is] always the most glamorous of mental diseases, since it seems to represent the insane's ideal of the normal. Just as the agnostic world keeps alive its religious festivals in order to satisfy the vacation needs of its

workforce, so when medical science has conquered all disease certain mental afflictions, schizophrenia chief among them, will be mimicked for social reasons' (*UGM* 278).

CHAPTER 3. THE DEATH OF AFFECT

1. In the late 1950s, at a time when he was working as an editor of the British periodical *Chemistry and Industry*, Ballard had already started to work on a novel made almost entirely of collaged excerpts from the US magazine, *Chemical Engineering News* (*R/S* 38).
2. Ballard's comments here bear an interesting relation to Ransom's vision, in *The Drought*, of the abandoned cars, whose sand-submerged shapes appear as a 'succession of humps, the barest residue of identity' transfigured by 'the essences of their own geometry' (*D*. 153–4).
3. Quoted in James Goddard and David Pringle (eds.), *J. G. Ballard: The First Twenty Years* (Hayes: Bran's Head, 1976), 26.

CHAPTER 4. AN ALPHABET OF WOUNDS

1. Ballard recently disavowed this statement, claiming that *Crash*, far from being 'a moral indictment of the sinister marriage between sex and technology', was in fact 'what it appears to be': 'a psychopathic hymn...but a psychopathic hymn which has a point' (Will Self, 'Conversations: J. G. Ballard', in *Junk Mail*, Penguin, London, 1996, p. 348).
2. Marshall McLuhan, *The Mechanical Bride: Folklore of Industrial Man* (Boston: Beacon, 1967), 94.
3. Another intriguing example of Ballard's tendency to mix the vocabularies of technology and religion occurs in a more recent article in which he defines neurobiology as 'Science's Sistine Chapel' (*UGM* 279).
4. Henry Adams, *The Education of Henry Adams* (Boston: Houghton Mifflin, 1961), 380.
5. Adams, *The Education of Henry Adams*, 381.
6. Filippo Tommaso Marinetti, *Selected Writings*, trans. R. W. Flint (London: Secker and Warburg, 1972), 40.
7. As critics have pointed out (see, for instance, D. Pringle, *Earth Is the Alien Planet: J. G. Ballard's Four-Dimensional Nightmare*, Borgo Press, San Bernardino, 1979, pp. 42–8, and G. Stephenson, *Out of the Night and Into the Dream: A Thematic Study of the Fiction of J. G. Ballard*, Greenwood Press, New York, 1991, pp. 79–80), Shakespeare's *The*

Tempest provides a useful model for an understanding of many of
Ballard's stories which explicitly or implicitly build upon the
interaction between a Prospero, a Miranda and a Caliban figure. As
Gregory Stephenson notes, each of the characters in Ballard's
version of the story in *Concrete Island* can be seen as playing a double
role. Whereas Jane Sheppard alternately acts the parts of the
innocent Miranda and the witch Sycorax, Proctor, whose behaviour
proves by turns destructive and benevolent, combines the baseness
and animality of Caliban with the ethereal grace of Ariel. For
Stephenson, Maitland's divided self enacts the roles of both
Antonio and Prospero, who is set adrift on the sea by his usurping
brother and washes up on a lonely island, just as Maitland is
brought to the traffic island by a car accident willed by his
unconscious self. Ballard's perverted treatment of motifs from *The
Tempest* is also apparent in the character bearing the name of
Miranda in *The Drought*, who reveals herself to be the antithesis of
the Shakespearean model of innocence and virginity.

8. Martin Amis, *Visiting Mrs Nabokov* (London: Penguin, 1993), 81.
9. David Pringle, *Earth Is the Alien Planet: J. G. Ballard's Four-
Dimensional Nightmare* (San Bernardino: Borgo Press, 1979), 42.
10. Pringle, *Earth Is the Alien Planet*, 46.

CHAPTER 7.   THE LOSS OF THE REAL

1. In an essay entitled, 'The Orders of the Simulacra', Baudrillard
writes: 'We live everywhere already in an "esthetic" hallucination
of reality. The old slogan "truth is stranger than fiction"...is
obsolete. There is no more fiction that life could possibly confront,
even victoriously – it is reality itself that disappears utterly in the
game of reality – radical disenchantment, the cool and cybernetic
phase following the hot stage of fantasy' (J. Baudrillard, *Simulations*,
trans. P. Foss, P. Patton and P. Beichman, Semiotext(e), New York,
1983, p. 148).

CHAPTER 8.   FROM SHANGHAI TO SHEPPERTON

1. Baudrillard, *Simulations*, trans. P. Foss, P. Patton and Philip
Beichman (New York: Semiotext(e), 1983), 146.
2. Roger Luckhurst's article 'Petition, Repetition and "Autobiography": J. G. Ballard's *Empire of the Sun* and *The Kindness of Women*'
(*Contemporary Literature*, 35:4, 1994, pp. 688–708) offers a more
detailed discussion of this blurring of boundaries between fictional

and autobiographical material. According to Luckhurst, Ballard's 'autobiographical' novels, far from deciphering the cryptic code of his work, further enhance the 'unreadability' of the earlier fiction. As a result of Ballard's 'positive valorization of "inauthenticity" and mediation', the 'primal scenes' of *Empire of the Sun* and *The Kindness of Women* are constantly restaged and recombined in 'fictions which yet teasingly and forever undecidedly play within the frame of the "autobiographical"' (*Contemporary Literature*, 35:4, 1994, p. 701).

3. Dennis A. Foster, 'J. G. Ballard's *Empire of the Senses*: Perversion and the Failure of Authority', *PMLA*, 108:3 (May 1993), 527.
4. Foster, 'J. G. Ballard's *Empire of the Senses*', 530.
5. Will Self, *Junk Mail* (London: Penguin, 1996), 360.

CHAPTER 9.   MORE NEWS FROM THE NEAR FUTURE

1. Nicholas Zurbrugg, *The Parameters of the Postmodern* (Carbondale and Edwardsville: Southern Illinois University Press, 1993), 143.
2. Zurbrugg, *The Parameters of the Postmodern*, 143–4.
3. Zurbrugg, *The Parameters of the Postmodern*, 143.
4. Will Self, *Junk Mail* (London: Penguin, 1996), 342.
5. Self, *Junk Mail*, 343.
6. Fredric Jameson, *Postmodernism, or The Cultural Logic of Capitalism* (London: Verso, 1991), 6.
7. Martin Amis, *Einstein's Monsters* (London: Penguin, 1988), 17.
8. Lukas Barr, 'Don't Crash: The J. G. Ballard Interview', *KGB* 7 ('KGB Media', 1995), available on the Internet: http://www.kgbmedia.com/wsv/ballard2.html.
9. Self, *Junk Mail*, 355.

CHAPTER 10.   REFLECTIONS IN PLACE OF A CONCLUSION

1. Theodor W. Adorno and Max Horkheimer, *Dialectic of Enlightenment* (London: Allen Lane, 1972), 3.
2. Quoted in Colin Greenland, *The Entropy Exhibition: Michael Moorcock and the British 'New Wave' in Science Fiction* (London: Routledge, 1983), 98.
3. Marshall McLuhan, *The Mechanical Bride: Folklore of Industrial Man* (Boston: Beacon, 1967), p. v.

Select Bibliography

WORKS BY J. G. BALLARD

Reference is to first publication.

The Wind from Nowhere (New York: Berkley, 1962; Harmondsworth: Penguin, 1967).

The Voices of Time (New York: Berkley, 1962). Short stories.

The Drowned World New York: Berkley, 1962; London: Gollancz, 1963).

The Four-Dimensional Nightmare (London: Gollancz, 1963). Short stories.

The Terminal Beach (London: Gollancz, 1964). Short stories.

The Burning World (New York: Berkley, 1964). Retitled: *The Drought* (London: Cape, 1965).

The Crystal World (London: Cape, 1966).

The Day of Forever (London: Panther, 1967). Short stories.

The Disaster Area (London: Cape, 1967). Short stories.

The Overloaded Man (London: Panther, 1967). Short stories.

The Atrocity Exhibition (London: Cape, 1970; revised, London: Flamingo, 1993). Retitled: *Love and Napalm: Export USA* (New York: Grove, 1972).

Vermilion Sands (New York: Berkley, 1971; London: Cape, 1973). Short stories.

Crash (London: Cape, 1973).

Concrete Island (London: Cape, 1974).

High-Rise (London: Cape, 1975).

Low-Flying Aircraft (London: Granada, 1976). Short stories.

The Unlimited Dream Company (London: Cape, 1979).

The Venus Hunters (London: Granada, 1980). Short stories.

Hello America (London: Cape, 1981).

Myths of the Near Future (London: Cape, 1982). Short stories.

Empire of the Sun (London: Gollancz, 1984).

The Day of Creation (London: Gollancz, 1987).

Running Wild (London: Century Hutchinson, 1988). Novella.

War Fever (London: William Collins, 1990). Short stories.

The Kindness of Women (London: HarperCollins, 1991).

Rushing to Paradise (London: Flamingo, 1994).

A User's Guide to the Millennium (London: Flamingo, 1996). Essays.

Cocaine Nights (London: Flamingo, 1996).

INTERVIEWS

Barber, L., 'Sci-Fi Seer', *Penthouse*, 5:5 (1970), 16–30.
Barr, L., 'Don't Crash: The J. G. Ballard Interview', *KGB*, 7 ('KGB Media', 1995), available on the Internet: http://www.kgbmedia.com/wsv/ballard2.html.
Frick, T., 'J. G. Ballard', *Paris Review*, 94 (1984), 132–60.
Goddard, J. and D. Pringle, 'Interview', in *J. G. Ballard: The First Twenty-Two Years* (Hayes, Middlesex: Bran's Head, 1976), 8–35.
Juno, A., and V. Vale., 'Interview with JGB', *RE/Search*, 8:9 (1984), 6–35.
Pringle, D., 'From Shanghai to Shepperton', *Foundation: The Review of Science Fiction*, 24 (1982), 5–23.
—— 'J. G. Ballard', *Interzone*, 106 (1996), 12–16.
Revell, G., 'Interview with JGB', *RE/Search*, 8–9 (1984), 42–52.
Self, W., 'Conversations: J. G. Ballard', in *Junk Mail* (London: Penguin, 1996), 329–71.

CRITICAL STUDIES

Baudrillard, J., 'Ballard's Crash', *Science Fiction Studies* (November 1991), 313–30. A celebration of *Crash* as a 'hyperreal' novel that eradicates traditional boundaries between fiction and reality. Argues that the 'radical functionalism' of Ballard's novel 'devours its own rationality' and therefore becomes an undefinable object, 'neither good nor bad: ambivalent'.
Bradbury, M., 'Unlimited Dreams', in *No, Not Bloomsbury* (London: André Deutsch, 1987), 346–8. A brief but suggestive response to *The Unlimited Dream Company*. Describes the novel as 'a dreamy pastoral, a fertile contradiction of the world of cement and iron' of Ballard's earlier novels.
Brigg, P., *J. G. Ballard* (Mercer Island, WA: Starmont House, 1985). A helpful introduction covering Ballard's work up to *Empire of the Sun*. Includes an annotated bibliography of selected criticism.
Foster, D. A., 'J. G. Ballard's Empire of the Senses: Perversion and the Failure of Authority', *PMLA*, 108:3 (May 1993): 519–32. An ambitious and controversial study of *Running Wild*, *Crash* and *Empire of the Sun* focusing on Ballard's tendency to describe a world motivated by perverse pleasure. Grounding his approach on an analysis of the relationship between technology, identity and death in Ballard's fiction, Foster argues that *Crash* 'demonstrates less how the perversion originates than the way it has become fully interwoven with the forms of advertising and technology that drive contemporary capitalism'.
Greenland, C., *The Entropy Exhibition: Michael Moorcock and the British*

'New Wave' in Science Fiction (London: Routledge, 1983). Contains an interesting account of Ballard's achievement in the context of the British New Wave school.

Luckhurst, R., *The Angle Between Two Walls: The Fiction of J. G. Ballard* (Liverpool: Liverpool University Press, 1997). A provocative, theoretically alert reading of Ballard's fiction within a series of philosophical and theoretical contexts ranging from Freud's *Beyond the Pleasure Principle* to Derrida's essays on Maurice Blanchot and the question of genre. Explores the uncertain terrain of the 'fictional and autobiographical pacts' that underlie Ballard's fiction. Contains a discussion of Ballard's 'double marginalization' as a science fiction writer and a cult author.

Menegaldo, G., 'De la dystopie à l'impossible utopie, ou des avatars de la science fiction chez J. G. Ballard (de "Chronopolis" à "The Ultimate City")', *Études anglaises*, 41:3 (1988), 291–306.

Pringle, D., *Earth is the Alien Planet: J. G. Ballard's Four-Dimensional Nightmare* (San Bernardino: Borgo Press, 1979). Pringle's study, though by now dated, still offers one of the most lucid and convincing examinations of Ballard's fiction up to *Low-Flying Aircraft*. Contains a brilliant discussion of Ballard's 'fourfold symbolism' and an analysis of his 'archetypal' characters that draws upon Jungian theory and Shakespeare's *The Tempest*.

—— *J. G. Ballard: A Primary and Secondary Bibliography* (Boston: G. K. Hall, 1984).

—— 'J. G. Ballard's Critical Coverage' (accessible at the URL: http://www.geocities.com/Area51/Corridor/4085). A regularly updated annotated bibliography of critical essays, reviews and books pertaining to Ballard's work.

Spinrad, N., 'The Strange Case of J. G. Ballard', in *Science Fiction and the Real World* (Carbondale and Edwardsville: Southern Illinois University Press, 1990), 182–97. An excellent overview of Ballard's career up to *The Day of Creation* by an American author who was himself associated with the New Wave school. Spinrad's approach is unusual, in that it centres on what the reception of Ballard's work tells us about the realities of SF and mainstream publishing on both sides of the Atlantic Ocean.

Stephenson, G., *Out of the Night and Into the Dream: A Thematic Study of the Fiction of J. G. Ballard* (New York: Greenwood Press, 1991). A perceptive, though perhaps too uncritical, study of the major themes of Ballard's fiction from the early short fiction to *Running Wild*. Stephenson's archetypal approach offers a detailed analysis of the patterns of psychic integration and transcendence embedded in Ballard's work.

Vale, V., and A. Juno (eds.), *RE/Search* 8–9 (1984). Special J. G. Ballard issue. Includes English translation of Ballard's oft-quoted Preface to the French edition of *Crash*.

Index